THE SIGN OF THE CROSS
THE GESTURE, THE MYSTERY, THE HISTORY

ANDREAS ANDREOPOULOS

PARACLETE PRESS
BREWSTER. MASSACHUSETTS·

The Sign of the Cross: The Gesture, the Mystery, the History

2006   First Printing

Copyright ©2006 by Andreas Andreopoulos

ISBN 10: 1-55725-496-6
ISBN 13: 978-1-55725-496-2

Library of Congress Cataloging-in-Publication Data
Andreopoulos, Andreas, 1966-
    The sign of the cross : the gesture, the mystery, the history /
    by Andreas Andreopoulos.
    p. cm.   ISBN-13: 978-1-55725-496-2
ISBN-10: 1-55725-496-6 1. Cross, Sign of the. 2. Crosses.
3. Jesus Christ--Crucifixion. I. Title.

BV197.5.A53 2006
242'.72--dc22

                                          2006023382

10 9 8 7 6 5 4 3 2 1

Published by Paraclete Press
Brewster, Massachusetts
www.paracletepress.com

Printed in the United States of America

This book is dedicated to the memory of my late grandfather
Fr. Andreas Andreopoulos (1888-1987)
to whom I owe all the spiritual quests and questions
with which I still struggle.
Without his prayers I would not be a theologian.

TABLE OF CONTENTS

FOREWORD

IX

INTRODUCTION

XIII

CHAPTER ONE

Experiencing the Sign of the Cross

1

CHAPTER TWO

The Sign of the Cross: Its History

11

CHAPTER THREE

The Need for Symbols and Signs

43

CHAPTER FOUR

A Prayer to Christ

84

CHAPTER FIVE

The Cosmic Cross

113

ACKNOWLEDGMENTS

139

FURTHER SUGGESTED READING

141

NOTES

143

INDEX

151

t my Orthodox church every Sunday I see families arrive at church and go up to the iconostasis, to greet the icon of the Lord. The parents stand before his searching gaze and make the sign of the cross fluidly: the right thumb and first two fingers together to recall the Trinity, and the last two fingers together and pressed down to the palm, to recall Christ's two natures and his descent to the earth. They touch forehead, abdomen, right shoulder, left shoulder, then sweep the right hand to the floor with a deep bow. After making two of these "metanias," they kiss Christ's hand, then make one more sign of the cross and a last bow.

With practice, what sounds like a very complicated ballet becomes second nature. Behind the parents come their children, who execute the same moves but have a shorter trip to reach the floor. And then there are the toddlers. If you're seated to the side, you can see a look of stern concentration come over the chubby face. Then there's a blur, as a tiny fist flies from ear to elbow to knee to nose, or just makes quick wobbly circles over the tummy. If these gestures were literally analyzed as to their symbolic meanings, they might be signaling heresies not yet imagined. But all this commotion is concluded by the little one's stretching up on tiptoe to kiss the hand of the all-compassionate man in the painting. That hand is giving a blessing; it is making the sign of the cross.

These children are doing what we all do to some extent: We take part in mysteries we can only partly comprehend. We do it within the safety of our Father's home, following in the footsteps of our elders.

In this case, the footsteps go back further than history can discover. It was in perhaps AD 204 that the brilliant North African writer Tertullian composed his essay "The Crown." He begins with a story then in the news: The Roman emperor had given laurel crowns to a band of victorious soldiers, but in the procession it was seen that one went bareheaded. When challenged by his tribune, he responded that he was not free to wear such a crown, because he was a Christian. At the time of Tertullian's writing the soldier was in prison awaiting martyrdom.

Tertullian tells us that some members of the local church were criticizing the soldier for rocking the boat; they had been enjoying a period of peace, and feared such boldness would provoke another bout of persecution. (Tertullian observed that they were no doubt already preparing to flee from one city to the next, since "that's all the gospel they cared to remember. . . ," adding tartly, "[T]heir pastors are lions in peace, deer in the fight.") But some retorted that nowhere is it written that Christians are forbidden to wear ceremonial crowns.

It is in responding to that challenge that Tertullian gives us an intriguing glimpse into the daily lives of early Christians. There are many things we Christians do, Tertullian says, that don't have a written mandate. In the Orthodox tradition, at baptism a person is immersed three times, after renouncing the devil, his pomp, and his angels. He makes a profession of faith "somewhat ampler . . . than the Lord has appointed in the Gospels." Christians receive the Eucharist only from the hand of the one presiding over the assembly. "If for these and other such rules, you insist on having positive Scripture injunction, you will find none. . . . The proper witness for tradition [is] demonstrated by long-continued observance."

Among the items that had had "long-continued observance," even at the dawn of Christian history, was the sign of the cross. "In all our travels and movements, in all our coming in and going out, in putting off our shoes, at the bath, at the table, in lighting our candles, in lying down, in sitting down, whatever employment occupies us, we mark our foreheads with the sign of the cross," Tertullian wrote.

It seems that the sign of the cross was such an entrenched element of Christian practice that a believer would not consider refraining from it. Tertullian believed it to be universal, and already ancient in AD 204.

I will leave Dr. Andreopoulos to fill in the story of how this sign came down to us today, and how its expression varied with time and place. His appealing book provides us not only with this history, but with many insights into the limitless, profound meaning of the sign of the cross. Yet, despite its mystery, the sign is a gesture simple enough for a child to adopt. The sign of the cross is a prayer in itself, one that is easy to include in the busy day—at the sound of an ambulance siren, as an expression of thanksgiving, as preparation for a difficult task, or on learning of a need for prayer.

It is my hope that this small book will acquaint many readers with a Christian custom that has roots deeper in the common history of our faith than anyone knows. The action may at first seem awkward; it may take time to acquire the gracefulness of those who have woven it through their prayers for decades. But there is hardly a more visible way to "take up your cross," as the Gospel of Matthew says (Matthew 10:38), than this, and join the company of those who in all ages have borne witness to Christ before the world.

Frederica Mathewes-Green

INTRODUCTION

I am writing this book as someone who grew up in the Orthodox faith: The sermons, the icons, the hymns, and the liturgical images from that tradition are inextricably linked with how I understand and express my spirituality. The subject of this book deserves a personal perspective as well as an academic one. As a professor of theology I am tempted to research and write about the sign of the cross in different times and places, keeping a critical distance and letting the readers form their own images and conclusions. Yet, as a practicing Orthodox Christian, who has grown up around icons and incense, I cannot write in a generic and flavorless way that might conceal how I am affected and moved by the symbols of the Orthodox Church.

I hope that people who grew up in different traditions will find it easy to relate to my experiences and feelings in the Orthodox Church, and sense a similarity to the experiences and feelings they receive in their own Churches. Yet, this book is also for the unchurched reader who wishes to understand the importance of the liturgical experience of the sign of the cross.

I am trying to avoid writing a book solely for my own religious community, especially since I believe that the ideas behind the curtain of these cultural and religious expressions could be understood and appreciated by a wider audience. For this reason, with the exception of the chapter on the historical development of the sign of the cross, I have tried to stay away from too many references to writings by the church Fathers and to hymns, which are second nature to the Orthodox. Instead, I have opted for a biblical level or reference, in order to open up the discussion to other readers, who will appreciate the firm biblical grounding of the Orthodox Church. This is also necessary for Orthodox readers, for the legacy of the church Fathers is given in order to serve the Bible and holy tradition, and therefore we start with the biblical text. As an eminent Orthodox theologian noted recently, sometimes Orthodox get fascinated with Mark the Ascetic and Isaac the Syrian, and they overlook Mark the Evangelist and Isaac the son of Abraham.

On the other hand, completely putting aside the legacy of writings by the church Fathers, as well as the customs and traditions of the church, one of which is the sign of the cross itself, would be senseless—a denial of the power and the divinity of the Holy Spirit. The Holy Spirit spoke through the prophets, as we recognize in the Creed, but also through the Fathers and the saints of the church. The teachings of the Fathers are present at every turn in this book, even when they are not mentioned by name.

The Bible is the foundation and also the product of the church; they both flow out of each other. This may sound a little out of touch in the contemporary world, because the Bible has been a constant throughout two millennia, uniting Churches with otherwise different customs and traditions. It is not possible to imagine a Christian Church without a biblical foundation.

On the other hand, Jesus did not come in the guise of a law-giver or a founding father; he did not produce a constitution or a body of written works that would end all subsequent arguments before they started. He established a church instead, a community of saints, which was defined by his Eucharistic body and nourished by the Holy Spirit. It is this church that, almost at the same time it was born, produced, selected, and set the canon for the authoritative writings that reveal Jesus in the church. So, in the end, the church and the Bible are different incarnations of the body of Christ, and as such their sanctity, significance, and authority are not only equal or similar, but are exactly of the same nature, which flows from Jesus himself.

Similarly, what unites the church of Christ is not specific to the local culture, but has its origins in heaven. The church includes the sum of the local expressions of the "Christly experience," and it transcends cultural expression. Therefore, as an Easterner I would be honored to see an American from Texas pray with icons, and I feel it would be perfectly normal for me to celebrate the feast of Gregory the Illuminator of Armenia, or to adopt the Celtic cross.

In the same way that the catholicity of the church has space for all external expressions of the faith, it is in this spirit that a book on the sign of the cross may be, as the sign itself, an offering of the East to the West (and in this case, the Catholic tradition, with its heart in Rome, is also to be considered "East").

With this in mind, I have kept traditionally "Orthodox" concepts and expressions that may not be immediately recognizable in the West, such as an eagerness to regard the iconography of the church as an equally valid source of theology as written sources. When I speak about the church building, I refer to the Byzantine church. When I speak about the Divine Liturgy, I refer to the Liturgy of St. John Chrysostom and the Liturgy of St. Basil the Great. All these belong to the entirety of Christendom. What unites us is much more than that which divides us, and although it would be premature to envision ecclesiastical unity, we have reached the time and place where we can all learn from each other.

The focal point of this small book is the sign of the cross, the physical gesture of "crossing oneself." In order to understand it, I approached the topic from a historical, liturgical, and symbolic perspective. As is the case with many religious symbols, the sign of the cross is connected with many of the mysteries of the faith.

The reader will not find much here about the cross or the sign of the cross as a symbol associated with suffering. There is enough literature on this aspect of the spirituality of the cross. Rather, I have oriented myself towards more ancient sources of inspiration, for which the image of the cross has a triumphant character. In this book I have tried to distance the sign of the cross from the kind of pietism that often undermines the true metaphysical dimensions of salvation through the cross of Jesus. I have included a history of the sign of the cross, an introduction to religious symbolism, a chapter on the sign of the cross in relation to the life of Jesus, and a discussion of the sign of the cross as a symbol of cosmic spirituality, which in turn reflects the personal sign of the cross.

One may start with the smallest symbol and end in the biggest theological questions that defy our logic. Very often, though, our entanglement with the big issues defines how we deal with the smaller ones. This is especially true in a church that has had to meld and integrate elements from its two-thousand-year-old tradition, combining them carefully in its liturgical canvas, where everything is connected with everything else.

I view this book as a journey in pursuit of the meaning of the sign of the cross, along with the various ideas, images, histories, and symbolisms connected with it. My hope is that this book contains enough historical information and theological commentary to satisfy the scholar of religion, yet with a more personal spiritual interest for the general reader to offer a synthetic view that helps form a larger picture.

Andreas Andreopoulos

THE SIGN OF THE CROSS
THE GESTURE, THE MYSTERY, THE HISTORY

CHAPTER ONE

EXPERIENCING
THE SIGN OF THE CROSS

My grandfather, Fr. Andreas Andreopoulos, was a priest. (In Orthodox Christianity, priests may marry before they are ordained.) I had a very close rapport with him. He taught me how to read and write before I went to school. This was our game: I still remember in the afternoons, when I was four, he would ask me to "fetch the book." The "book" was an old, dated, decrepit grade-one reading text that had not been used in the school system for over a decade, but somehow found its way into my grandfather's belongings. And he trusted me with it.

The old man, impressive with his long white beard and his priestly garments, well in his eighties at the time, would then proceed to teach me the letters of the alphabet, words and phrases, which I absorbed so fast that by the age of five I could read as well as any adult. This learning game of ours is one of my earliest and fondest memories.

The old man loved to tell me stories from his adventurous past, mostly from the 1922 war with Turkey where he survived by a miracle. As the Greek army was withdrawing, he was saved at the battlefield by an officer who happened to know him and put my grandfather atop his horse. He also liked telling me stories from the *Odyssey* and the *Iliad*, from the Chronicle of Alexander the Great and from the ancient past. Before any other stories, these were told to me first.

Only later were stories from the life of Jesus and the Bible added. Having learned to read at such an early age, I was quickly given books and was left alone to devour them, something that could not have pleased me more.

The stories from the pagan and the Christian past continued, but as I grew older and started going to school, there was less time for me to spend with my grandfather. I did not notice it then, but gradually there was less talking and more doing. Instead of listening to tales of the past, I was taught how to pray, how to cross myself, how to identify the parts of the church and the saints on the walls of the richly decorated church of St. Barbara, where my grandfather celebrated the liturgy.

I still remember how he taught me the sign of the cross: "Here, Andriko. Three fingers together, like this. Three fingers, for the Holy Trinity. Now we cross ourselves from the forehead, to the breast, to our right shoulder, to our left shoulder (and then we pat our belly). It is in rhythm: Father, Son, and Holy Spirit."

As the old man performed the gesture, so did I, following suit in style and rhythm. This was the first encounter with the sign of the cross that I remember well (my first unremembered encounter being when I was baptized and the sign was made over me many times during the ritual.)

Sometimes my grandfather would take me inside the altar of the church during the liturgy. This experience was so powerful that it has overshadowed my early impressions of normal church life, and therefore my memories of the altar precede my memories of the nave, the main part of the church. The fragrances, the faces of the saints in the icons, the priestly vestments, everything was so amplified there, whereas in the nave people very often ignored the liturgy and talked to each other casually, as if they had simply met in the street.

I was too young to understand the words of the liturgy or the significance of the rituals, but somehow taking all this inside me, internalizing it, seemed natural, like being introduced to a practice that was somehow already familiar to me.

And the cross was everywhere. Greek churches fashion a huge cross at the back of the altar, which altar boys and priests kiss every time they pass by. The wall icons were not framed, but separated from each other by decorative designs, often by many small crosses that blended into each other. The impressive, colorful, and glistening liturgical vestments of my grandfather and the other priests also reprised this: Some were decorated with many miniscule crosses, sometimes with prominent crosses. Some crosses were so subtle that to most they remained unnoticed.

Within the church, there was no place the cross was not represented. Very often during the liturgy, priests and lay people would cross themselves en masse. Later I discovered that this happened mostly at the beginning or at the end of something important—such as a prayer or the Gospel reading—or whenever something especially important was mentioned, such as the Trinity; the Theotokos, the Mother of God; or even the saint of the day.

Yet, there are instances when I do not understand why people cross themselves other than, as Tevye from *Fiddler on the Roof* would say, "It's a tradition that nobody knows how it started, but it is tradition nonetheless!"

This practice of the sign of the cross was not restricted to liturgy. We crossed ourselves before meals. At lunchtime, when the entire family was summoned, my grandfather always blessed the food, and when I was old enough to learn it by heart, I recited the Lord's Prayer. We all crossed ourselves at the beginning and at the end of the blessing. Sometimes a second prayer was recited at the end of the meal, and naturally it involved additional crossing.

Prayer was something interwoven with social and family life and activities. The sign of the cross was an indispensable part of these activities. But even when there was no time for a proper prayer, for example in the beginning of a journey, the sign of the cross would suffice, being the simplest symbol of prayer and request. Interestingly, ancient writers noted that during prayer the shape one's body takes forms the figure of a cross.[1] In ancient Christianity as well as in pagan religions people prayed extending or lifting their hands, as priests still do today.

Here is what is so fascinating about the sign of the cross: its simplicity. A cross is how illiterate people sign a document, because it is the simplest recognizable sign they can draw, signifying their acquiescence to an official form. And though the cross is perhaps one of the simplest things in Christian ritual, it clearly connects with some of the greatest Christian mysteries. The Incarnation, the Resurrection, and the Second Coming were narrative events that my childish mind had no difficulty accepting with a simple explanation.

It stood to reason that if God loved us, he could come down to earth, that he could not be killed without rising from the dead, and that some day he would come again. With some of the more abstract or more enigmatic parts of the faith, this proved to be more difficult. And even now, writing as a professor of theology, I have to admit that what puzzled me most as a child still puzzles me today: The Crucifixion, the self-sacrifice and death of God, and the riddle given to me by my grandfather at the same time he "gave" me the sign of the cross: "Father, Son, and Holy Spirit, a trinity consubstantial and indivisible."

Here I have to say that the sign of the cross is one of the most fascinating elements of ritual symbolism. The most profound and incomprehensible mysteries are connected with such simple objects or symbols, which somehow manage to evoke them immediately, at an impulse, a gesture. An icon of a saint, for example, may express in just a few daring lines what requires volumes to be explained verbally. Likewise, performing a gesture on a regular basis may do a lot more for one's spiritual disposition than reading an entire library of books. Most likely, this is how some of those simple symbols became established and then were accepted. Perhaps the symbol that combines simplicity and profound meaning to a greater extent than any other symbol is the sign of the cross.

Where did this symbol and practice begin? Neither the cross as a symbol nor the practice of crossing oneself were given to us in a direct way by Jesus himself—unlike, for instance, the sacrament of Communion, which Jesus directly instituted. Nor was the sign of the cross in popular use among the earliest Christians. Though some biblical background supports the importance of the cross as a religious symbol (most explicitly in Saint Paul's assertion in first Corinthians that "we preach Christ crucified"), it would more likely have appeared as an objectionable symbol to the Roman world, similar to how an electric chair, a noose, or another violent instrument of execution would appear to us.

In the days of the early church, Christians were fond of other symbols of recognition, similarly ritually charged, such as the famous symbol of the fish that, recently rediscovered, can be found pasted on many cars driven by Christians. Despite the ritual history of the fish, there is little visual symbolic power to it—it serves as a reminder of the acrostic *Jesus Christ, Son of God, Savior,* which in Greek happens to spell "fish." The fish was eventually surpassed by the cross as a visual symbol. The simplicity and the archetypal power of the cross made it popular.

One exceptional factor explains why the cross overshadowed all other symbols of Christianity: The cross could be performed as a simple and immediately recognizable gesture. Many ancient writers refer to the "sign of the cross" even when they mean any physical cross, even a crossroads, and not only in reference to the cross of Christ. The importance of the physicality of the symbol may not be something that naturally occurs to us, used as we are to our literate Western world. But very few people in late antiquity and the Middle Ages could read and write, and therefore few could appreciate or internalize something as complex as an acrostic. However, Christianity in the early stages of development did not spread so much through the upper social circles of learned theologians and philosophers as through the lower socioeconomic strata: fishermen, carpenters, tanners, and slaves. The common people took their catechism seriously, and expressed their religious faith much better with a prayer and a gesture than through daily reading.

No conclusive evidence points to a date or place for adopting the cross as a symbol, although possibly the cross was already in use during apostolic times. We see traces of the symbol appearing in the second century, in the writings of Justin Martyr, Tertullian, and Irenaeus of Lyons. Eventually adopted as a symbol of historic, spiritual, and liturgical significance, the cross came into use as Christianity grew and matured. Theologians explored the mystery of the death of Jesus Christ, remembering the actual cross on which he died. Then suddenly, in the fourth century, the cross became the established symbol.

In the fourth century the search for the True Cross led Helen, the mother of the emperor Constantine the Great, to Jerusalem, where she discovered Jesus' cross by its miraculous healing power. The discovery and raising (or Exaltation) of the True Cross by the patriarch Makarios of Jerusalem is now, more than fifteen centuries later, an important feast day of the church. The reasons for the veneration that quickly followed may be difficult to understand by today's standards. But pilgrims began to flock from all over the world to see this valuable relic whose cult started assuming idolatrous proportions.

But at almost the same time as this spread of the worship of the actual materials of the cross, a more spiritual interpretation of the Cross and the Crucifixion was being developed in the desert. The early martyrs such as Saint Stephen, who were witnesses of the divinity of Jesus, were succeeded in the Christian Empire by monastics. The monastics—monks, nuns, or ascetics—who lived in the desert, sometimes in religious communities, sometimes alone, sacrificed themselves, or rather *crucified* themselves to the world, following the example of Jesus. In this way they began to bring into spiritual truth the nature of the cross. The sign and symbol of the cross were understood among them not so much in relation to the historic relic, but as the archetype of the crucifixion of the self, of their own humility and surrender of the will and of the self—the ascetic way to subjugate the passions of the body and the soul. This simple symbol fulfilled the spiritual need of the early church for a reminder of Jesus' historic and willful death for humankind. This symbol also was raised up for those who wished to leave the world behind them and fight demons in the desert.

Perhaps the aspect of Christianity that more than others transmitted the significance of the cross to common people was the ritual tradition. The church provided Christians with a systematic method to transform the secular world into a spiritual world, via liturgical practice and signs and symbols within tradition. The liturgy has developed, to a great extent, around the image of the cross. Both in ancient times and now, the cross is the final image of the liturgy. This suggests that Christians, after participating in the Eucharist, the sacramental body and blood of Jesus, should go out into the world and "bear their cross," as followers of Christ.

The basilica, the Roman public building adopted for use by early churches, was replaced in the East by a church building in the shape of a cross. This shape was also reflected in the way liturgical services were celebrated. Even now, this cruciform liturgical structure is seen in Eastern churches and monasteries, where the axis from the entrance to the altar of the church is supplanted by the axis between the two choirs (the semi-domes on the left and right of a church where sometimes two choirs or chanters are placed). The church building in this form represents the entire universe, heaven and earth. And the liturgical processions during several services on the West-East axis as well as the antiphons on the North-South axis mark this representation of the universe with the sign of the cross.

The sign of the cross developed alongside the cruciform sign of blessing with which most Christians are familiar. Both liturgical life and icons point to the cross. This sign, made as a gesture, acquired several meanings as it developed and was performed by bishops and priests. However, lay people use the sign of the cross as their own gesture of blessing when they bless food or when they bless each other. Within one movement, this puts into perspective the significance to the religious life of the sign of the cross: It encompasses historical memory, prayer, ascesis, and blessing.

Delving deeper into Christian tradition, we keep finding ways that the theology and the symbolism of the cross are integrated and reflect many aspects of Christianity. This book's particular exploration, however, tries to translate the significance of the cross into something personal and immediate.

When we trace the cross on our body, we actively invite it—we *become* the cross.

The difference between understanding the mystery of the cross and performing this simple gesture is perhaps as big as the gap between knowing what is right and practicing it. It may not have the same importance in each Christian denomination, but wherever the gesture is practiced, it says, "I am a Christian. I invoke the power and the mercy of the cross of Christ, and I try to sanctify myself and to live keeping in mind the sacrifice of Jesus and the mystery of the Father, the Son, and the Holy Spirit." This practice and the implications go through my mind when I cross myself. Just as my grandfather taught me.

CHAPTER TWO

THE SIGN OF THE CROSS
ITS HISTORY

The origins of the sign of the cross are lost in the unwritten tradition of the church. Our information is sparse because this ancient practice emerged naturally, as something that made sense to most Christians. Nevertheless, tracing its historical development allows us to better understand what the sign of the cross expresses and its importance for those who perform the gesture.

In the fourth century Basil of Caesarea wrote, "The doctrines and the kerygmata [teachings] that are preserved in the church are given to us in two different ways: the doctrines are given to us in written teachings, and the kerygmata have been given to us secretly, through the apostolic tradition. . . . To start with the first and the most common among them, who has ever taught us in writing the sign of the cross, which signifies our hope in our Lord Jesus Christ?"[2] The observation of Basil, this erudite bishop of the early church, rings out like a warning in our pursuit of the history of the sign of the cross: This sign was a custom of the church that nobody had reason to defend or explain, a tradition seen as ancient by the fourth century, and for this reason most of what is important about it was never put to writing.

Throughout Christian history, the sign of the cross was rarely an object of study. Most of the information we gather comes from periods of crisis, during which people felt the need to explain what should have been obvious to everyone.

Similarly, despite Basil's implicit warning, this book examines and illumines the historical development of the sign of the cross in the life of the church, so that what is obvious to a practitioner may be understood by outsiders (as much as one can understand a spiritual practice from without).

Basil expresses a view that has changed little over the centuries. The sense of "tradition" in the church implies a tacit acceptance of what has been handed down to us from the past. Yes, there are certain traditions that have accidentally become corrupt and need to return to their original meaning, or traditions evolving because the world is now ready to accept them. But those are more theological, academic views of the issue. For others, the millions of people who pray and worship God every day, this matter is not complicated. Every child who goes to church picks up naturally what people do there, adopts it as a way to express his spirituality, and passes it on to the next generation. The image of many people performing the sign of the cross at the same time in church, or the image of an old man who, scared by a sudden noise, traces the sign of the cross on his body, show how powerful this tradition is for many people.

We do not know much about how the gesture of the sign of the cross in the ancient church was performed. The simplest way to perform it would have been to trace it over the forehead with one finger, most likely the thumb—since some priests still "seal their forehead" in this manner before reading the Gospel. The sign over the forehead, sometimes in the form of an X, is confirmed in early icons and coins, suggesting a standard way to cross oneself. Tertullian, a learned and influential writer of the second and third century, mentions this in one of the earliest testimonies we have about the sign of the cross, where he writes:

> At every forward step and movement, at every going in and out, when we put on our clothes and shoes, when we bathe, when we sit at the table, when we light the lamps, on the couch, on the seat, in all the ordinary actions of daily life, we trace upon the forehead the sign.[3]

We may imagine the early Christians, emerging from the age of persecutions, some of them having suffered or lost family members as martyrs, and some having been baptized or initiated into Christianity by a saint, giving their entire lives to Christianity. The sign of the cross was performed over everything they wished to consecrate—their food, their pillow, and each other.

The sign of the cross was a blessing so necessary to them, in a time when the world was turning upside down. And in this chaotic time, Christians chose to bless themselves with the sign of Christ. The few witnesses to this from the early church suggest how immediately widespread this gesture must have been, and how important in the everyday life of Christians.

Like Tertullian, who wrote about the sign over the forehead, St. Cyril of Jerusalem wrote about the sign of the cross in the fourth century:

Let us then not be ashamed to confess the Crucified. Let the cross as our seal, be boldly made with our fingers upon our brow and on all occasions; over the bread we eat, over the cups we drink; in our comings and in our goings; before sleep; on lying down and rising up; when we are on our way, and when we are still. It is a powerful safeguard; it is without price, for the sake of the poor; without toil, because of the sick; for it is a grace from God, a badge of the faithful, and a terror to the devils; for "he displayed them openly, leading them away in triumph by force of it." For when they see the Cross, they are reminded of the Crucified; they fear him who has "smashed the heads of the dragons." Despise not the seal as a free gift, but rather for this reason honor your benefactor all the more.[4]

The idea of a sign made on the forehead did not originate with Christianity. References to a sign, or rather to a mark on the forehead, appear in the Old Testament as well as in other pre-Christian civilizations. Cain was perhaps the first person in history to associate his name with a mark on the forehead. In the book of Genesis, God makes a mark on Cain (and biblical scholars assign the place of the mark as the forehead) identifying Cain as someone who has killed, and also as someone being protected from being killed.

Similar references are found throughout the Old Testament. A sign on the forehead, and sometimes also on the hands, is a sign of castigation, a way to set aside a sinner.

This is reflected in the ninth chapter of Ezekiel where God commanded, "Go through the midst of the city, through the midst of Jerusalem, and set a mark upon the foreheads of the men who sigh and who cry because of all the abominations that are done in the midst thereof." Even a sore on the forehead could mark a person as unclean, as chapter 14 of Leviticus suggests. There is no mention of a mark on the forehead in the New Testament, except in the book of Revelation, where such a mark sometimes appears as a sign of the people of God, but also as a sign of the Antichrist.

The mark on the forehead as we see it in the Old Testament and in the Book of Revelation reveals something spiritually significant about the person who bears that mark, usually declaring something about the spiritual condition or identity of that person. The mark on the forehead is something like a "reading," an exposition of what this person is really like inside, as God sees him or her. Unlike a gesture or sign on the forehead, the mark is something permanent. The forehead is chosen as the most conspicuous place of display. In later Hellenistic Platonist and Neoplatonist tradition, which identified the mind with the true self, the forehead could be connected with the mind, but this connection does not bear out in the biblical tradition, where the heart and not the mind is identified as the center of the human being, the true self.

In the Old Testament, the mark on the forehead is given by God, even though the Old Testament references suggest a negative connotation. The book of Revelation treats the mark as one might a military insignia or a flag, as a means of identification, in this case identifying oneself with the side of God or with the side of the beast in the apocalyptic war.

Keeping this in mind, the act of tracing a sign on one's forehead reprises or rather anticipates the mark given by God. Interestingly, according to chapters 14 and 22 in the book of Revelation, the sign on the forehead is nothing other than the name of God, nothing other than the Hebrew letter *tau*, which was written as a cross. Although *tau* is not one of the letters used in spelling the name of God, it was seen as a symbol of God since it is the last letter in the Hebrew alphabet. *Tau* was viewed as the end, the completion and the perfection of all things, after which there is nothing else, and so it was viewed as a symbol of God in Jewish culture.

The early church writer Origen studied the Hebrew tradition extensively and gave this testimony: "[The letter *tau*] bears a resemblance to the figure of the Cross; and this prophecy (Ezek. ix. 4) is said to regard the sign made by Christians on the forehead, which all believers make whatsoever work they begin upon, and especially at the beginning of prayers, or of holy readings."[5]

Origen suggests the possibility of thinking of the Christian version of the sign both as a cross, and also as an X, after the Greek letter *chi* which is the first letter in the Greek word Χριστός (Christ), the specifically Christian equivalent of the name of God. The Hebrew *tau*, the Greek *chi* and the sign of the cross would have looked similar when traced on the forehead, as they are all performed with two movements of the hand. The X and the cross likely appeared at the same time in different parts of the Christianized Roman Empire.

Origen, writing in the third century, is clearly aware of the sign on the forehead as the sign of the cross. On the other hand, the use of the sign of the initial of Christ was still in effect in the fourth century: Early Christian images, such as the mosaics of the Piazza Armerina in Agrigento, Italy, which date from the time of Diocletian, as well as other early Christian artifacts, represent Christians with an X on their forehead.[6]

Tertullian, who writes, "We make the sign," may be referring to the sign of the cross or to the sign of the name of Christ. Even earlier, Justin Martyr, the great Christian apologist of the second century who connected the Bible with the Hellenistic tradition and Plato with Moses, connects the symbol of the cross with the pagan philosophical tradition, making no distinction between the cross proper and the X.[7]

The use of the cross as a sign has also had political implications, especially when we consider the vision and the actions of the Emperor Constantine the Great in the early fourth century.[8] Eusebius of Caesarea, the biographer of Constantine, attests that a great luminous cross appeared in the sky, with the inscription "Conquer by this," the day before an important battle. Seen in battle by Constantine and his troops, the cross was adopted immediately as an imperial military symbol.

Although Eusebius writes about the celebrated vision of Constantine referring to a luminous cross in the sky, the imperial insignia Constantine introduced also included the Greek letters X and P, which spell the name of Christ in Greek. It is possible that Constantine did this to point to the exact meaning of the cross. In conjunction with the name of Christ, the cross would be seen as a Christian symbol, even by people who did not know much about Christianity. In this way, both the cross and the Christogram (a combination of letters that form an abbreviation for the name of Jesus Christ) were promoted in the symbolism of that era via flags, coins, and other symbols, as though they were interchangeable. Quite likely, both symbols were understood and accepted in connection with each other. We have no reason to assume that Constantine was interested in instituting a specific symbolism; his interest seemed to be in showing that a Christian identity was evident.

This interest in a "Christian identity" may seem distant from us, but the conversion of Constantine and the legalization of the Christian religion was an event that shook the world of Christians. Since the death of Jesus on the cross, Christianity had suffered continuous persecution. Yet, against all odds, this persecuted minority spread its spiritual message to the ends of the powerful Roman Empire, converting even its persecutors. Nevertheless, this change occurred suddenly, as far as most Christians could see.

Nobody could anticipate the vision and the conversion of the head of the state, and for some Christians it was difficult to believe that the emperor had become a defender of Christianity. This change in the personal faith of the emperor eventually brought about a change in the entire empire, a change fully accomplished within a few generations.

To appreciate the magnitude of this transition and the importance of the Christian identity, we can try to imagine something similar in our culture. When, after World War II, Eastern Europe fell under the power of the USSR, this meant more than a political alliance. The national symbols of these countries often included the hammer and sickle and photographs of Soviet leaders. Russian became a second language or culture for many populations in the satellite states. National and cultural heritage were filtered to a great extent through party ideology. In other words, in only seventy years, a political condition changed not only the lives but also the sense of identity of millions of people. The change that occurred in the fourth century in the Roman Empire, where the emperor had been worshiped as a god for centuries, would be difficult to understand by many people. The Empire had to eventually redefine its identity, its laws, and its world view. The pursuit of a "Christian identity" through a Christian flag was only the beginning.

We have already looked at the sign of the cross and the letter *tau*, which in the Jewish tradition symbolized God, the letter that was written as a cross. But the first letter of the Hebrew alphabet was *aleph*, and this was written as an X in Hebrew as well as in Aramaic. These two letters are closely connected in Jewish theology.

"Truth" was seen as the most complete perfection, carried through to the identification of *truth* with *Christ* in many Gospel passages, especially in the Gospel of John, where Jesus himself says, "I am the way, the truth, and the life. No one comes to the Father except through me." The Hebrew word for truth is *emet*, spelled *aleph-mem-tau*, the first, middle and last letters of the alphabet. The cultural equivalent of *aleph* and *tau* in the Hellenistic culture prevalent during the time of the writing of the Gospels is *alpha* and *omega*, the first and last letters of the Greek alphabet. The same letters are identified with the person of Jesus in the book of Revelation. The *alpha* and the *omega* have become a standard insignia in iconic depictions of Jesus as the Pantokrator, or King of Majesty, and are used in early Christian monograms of Christ.

The *alpha* and the *omega*, as also the *aleph* and the *tau*, symbolize the beginning and the end, the absolute, and perfection. In this context, the cross and the X are fused into a single symbol that is not solely the *aleph* or solely the *tau*, but both at the same time.

After this symbolism became Hellenized in the *alpha* and the *omega*, most Christians were aware of this symbolism and of the connection between the cross and the X. But the early Christian communities certainly knew it very well. This is why the X appeared as an alternate form of performing the sign of the cross only in early Christianity. Jesus Christ was the truth, the *alpha* and the *omega*, the *aleph* and the *tau*. In his person the *alpha* and the *omega*, or the X and the cross, were fused; he is the beginning and the end at the same time, the manifestation of the absolute and perfection.

If not since the time of Origen, at least by the time of Cyril of Jerusalem, the significance of the sign had switched securely from the name of Jesus Christ to the symbol of the cross, while the Hebrew letters receded to the background and were forgotten. Soon, a little later in the West, Augustine seemed to deny any other significance to the sign, other than the cross of Christ: "And lastly, as every one knows, what else is the sign of Christ but the cross of Christ? For unless that sign be applied, whether it be to the foreheads of believers, or to the very water out of which they are regenerated, or to the oil with which they receive the anointing chrism, or to the sacrifice that nourishes them, none of them is properly administered."[9] From a modern perspective, this observation seems slightly strange. Augustine's question "what else is the sign of Christ but the cross of Christ?" is obviously rhetoric, but even so it does not make sense unless he is harking back to a previous historical idea, drawing readers into this new understanding. His question suggests that in another time, not too far back, the sign had been a reference either to the cross or to the name of Christ. Nevertheless, Augustine, by closing the matter, was also the last one to witness this alternate meaning. There was no doubt as to the meaning of the sign of the cross in the next wave of theology and practice connected to it.

The gesture of the sign of the cross was carried fully in the fourth century into the emergence of monasticism, which helped proliferate the use of the sign of the cross on the forehead. Although Anthony is often regarded as the father of monasticism, it was another Egyptian monk, Pachomius, who according to the tradition of the desert received instructions from an angel and organized the young monks into an order, laying down the rules that became the basis for all subsequent monastic orders in the East and the West.

Pachomius' organizational style was very much military, and the symbol of the cross became the identifying mark of this army of God. Pachomius "prescribed for the monks napless cowls, as for children, on which he ordered an imprint, the mark of a cross, to be worked in dark red."[10] Monastic life was in many ways the life of the cross, and it was natural for them to see their spiritual ascent as an imitation of the sacrifice of Jesus on his cross. As we can see in the numerous writings that describe the life of the monks of the desert, they saw the symbol and the sign of the cross as one of the strongest weapons against demons and temptations.[11] By placing the sign of the cross on their foreheads they reminded themselves that they were crucified to the world, and that their every action was done in the name of the cross. Egyptian monks wore the mark of the cross on their forehead, as a reprise of the identifying mark of God mentioned in the book of Revelation, and as the sign of the cross of Christ.

When exactly the transition occurred from the sign on the forehead (or on other parts of the body, such as the heart or the mouth) to the long cross, performed over the body, in the "larger" way with which we are familiar today, no one knows. But it is this "large" cross that transformed what was almost a private gesture into a gesture of public declaration. Several modern writers, following a Catholic Encyclopedia article on this topic written in 1907 by Herbert Thurston, suggest that the large cross is related to the profession of the two natures of Jesus, and therefore the shift took place against the background of the

Monophysitic crisis,[12] in the fifth and sixth centuries. The need for the large cross, the article suggests, was to demonstrate that the two fingers employed to make the sign were now much more visible than before. And the use of two fingers had become standardized as a response to the Monophysitic crisis, the article suggests.

There are two ancient sources though, that disprove this position. First, the testimony of Cyril of Jerusalem mentions the use of "fingers" without making any fuss about how many fingers are used and why—suggesting that this issue was not controversial or divisive at the time. This testimony predates the Monophysitic issue by at least one century. Cyril's detailed and sophisticated sermon on the importance of the Crucifixion disregarded the number of fingers used in making the sign of the cross, remaining unconcerned with the issues that Thurston believed were influential at the time.

Also, a long time after the discussion on the natures of Jesus had been put to rest, the sign of the cross was still performed on the forehead. John of Damascus writes in the eighth century: "[The cross] was given to us as a sign on the forehead, just as circumcision was given to Israel. For by it we the faithful are recognized and we separate ourselves from the unfaithful."[13] Long after the Monophysitic, Monoenergist and Monothelite heresies that questioned the nature of Christ were put to rest, John of Damascus still pointed to the sign of the cross performed on the forehead.[14] If Thurston's claim about the standardization of the two fingers and the shift to the large cross as an immediate result of the controversy on the natures of Christ in the fifth and sixth centuries was a claim made in error, what, if not a response to monophysitism, caused these changes?

As mentioned above, Cyril of Jerusalem writes that the sign is performed "with the fingers." It is anybody's guess whether the sign in his time was performed using two or three fingers, or even the entire hand. The particular piece of writing where Cyril writes about this is in his 13th Catechesis, dedicated entirely to the crucifixion of Jesus. That Cyril does not discuss the symbolism of the fingers suggests that the issue was not very charged at his time, that the symbolism was relatively simple.

Even while Cyril did not focus on the number of fingers, but only the gesture, one piece of historical note supports the use of two fingers: The Roman gesture for public speech consisted of a hand with these two fingers extended, and this gesture was passed on to Christianity. Still another piece of information reveals a different order.

John Chrysostom, slightly later than Cyril of Jerusalem, writes that "you should not just trace the cross with your finger, but you should do it in faith."[15] John clearly refers to the sign of the cross performed with one finger, probably the thumb or the index finger. And while the Antiochean background of John Chrysostom places him in the same part of the Roman world as Cyril of Jerusalem (and therefore we could not argue that they express different local customs), yet the two Fathers give us conflicting statements.

Because the early Fathers do not give precise or consistent information, it is possible that the early church attached no particular developed symbolism to the number of fingers used to trace the sign of the cross. Much later, Peter of Damascus attests to the use of two extended fingers, symbolizing the two natures of Christ:

> The holy Fathers have handed down to us the meaning of this holy sign, in order to refute heretics and unbelievers. The two fingers and the one hand then, represent the crucified Lord Jesus Christ, whom we profess as having two natures in one person. The right hand recalls his unlimited might and his sitting at the right hand of the Father. And one begins to trace it from above because of his descent from the heavens to us on earth. Furthermore, the movement of the hand from the right side to the left drives away the enemies and indicates that the Lord through his invincible might has conquered the devil who is on the left, a powerless and gloomy being.[16]

Peter provides the first clear report on the details of performing the sign of the cross. What caused him, at this point in time, to provide a detailed description and interpretation? Long settled was the issue of the two natures of Christ, so we may look for other reasons. One plausible explanation comes naturally to the foreground if we consider what John, the other theologian of Damascus, wrote about the sign of the cross. In the previously mentioned passage, John wrote that the sign of the cross was given to believers "just as circumcision was given to Israel. For by it we the faithful are recognized and we separate ourselves from the unfaithful."

Both John and Peter lived under the Muslim rule, although with a difference of four centuries between them (John of Damascus lived in the eighth century, while Peter of Damascus, while traditionally believed to have lived around the same time, most likely lived in the twelfth century). Muslims, as sources from that time attest, lift one finger when they ask God for forgiveness. John, who sees the sign of the cross as something that differentiates Christians from the unfaithful, and Peter, who dictates that the sign should be performed with two fingers, respond to the Muslim gesture of using one finger. This may explain why the custom of a priest crossing his forehead with his thumb has survived only in the West, which did not live under the political and religious threat of Islam. Imagine the struggling Christian community in the midst of expanding Muslim armies, as Christians tried to keep their identity and their faith, while everything around them changed. Christians kept the traditions of their forefathers, avoiding cultural and religious integration into the mainstream Muslim culture. So the sign of the two fingers not only professed the Christian faith, but also formed a call to preserve the Christian identity.

Something else particularly interesting in Peter's passage is his description of the sign of the cross formed from above to below and from right to left. This note suggests that Peter had the large cross in mind, shaped over the entire body, as it would not have been easy to picture and give much importance to minimized movements, barely seen.

Since John of Damascus refers to the sign on the *forehead,* the shift from the sign on the forehead to the sign over the body would have occurred after the eighth century, for reasons other than a reaction to the Monophysitic heresy. But if the shift to the large cross took place sometime between the eighth and the twelfth century, what brought it about?

Let's turn once more to the surrounding culture, and see what else was going on in the life of the symbols. One of the most turbulent periods in the life of the church happened in the eighth and ninth centuries when a theological dispute about the status, the meaning, and the significance of icons of Jesus, the saints, and angels used for veneration, divided the Byzantine Empire into two camps: the enemies of icons, called iconoclasts, and the defenders of icons, called iconophiles. The war on icons and iconophiles was waged by the emperor Leo III in 726, and continued by his son, Constantine V. Although it is still unclear why these emperors attacked an accepted and popular practice, one reasonable explanation points to these military emperors trying to understand why God no longer granted victory to the Christian armies, but that a significant Muslim expansion had moved through the Middle East. Persians and Arabs had conquered lands formerly belonging to the Roman-Byzantine Empire.

In seeing the differences between Christianity and Islam, what became obvious even to the rough soldiers rising through the ranks to become commanders, generals, and emperors, was that Muslims followed the biblical prohibition of icons, a prohibition that had been gradually put aside among Christians.

If God indeed was showing his anger for this blasphemy, while at the same time allowing the expansion of the Muslims who did not venerate or tolerate icons, perhaps God was indirectly pointing to the blasphemy of the Christians. The worship of icons, which even by the admission of the church had veered dangerously close to idolatry, was viewed as the problem. In quick succession, edicts forbidding the use of icons were issued. Sadly, many icons were destroyed, the defenders of icons arrested and tortured.

Among those defending icons were clergy and monastics, who developed sophisticated theological arguments explaining how and why icons formed an essential aspect of worship. By 843, the defenders of icons had prevailed, but the iconoclastic period left its mark in many aspects of Byzantine liturgy, theology, iconography, and worship.

Perhaps it is difficult for the Western reader to appreciate the reason for what could be called the war of icons. Nevertheless, worship and theological expression through icons are still important and living elements of the Eastern Church. A Western visitor who enters an Eastern church may be struck by the wall-to-wall iconography that extends all the way to the dome, leaving no space without an icon or a connecting design. Icons are often addressed during the liturgy, as if they are persons, and are also kept in "prayer corners" in homes.

Beyond theological and historical explanations of the use of icons, the faithful connect to the community of saints and the fellowship of God through icons. I remember how the faces of these strict yet calm saints and martyrs were looking at me when I was a child in church. Every time I responded to their gaze that seemed to come from a place beyond space and time, I did something more than learn their history: I learned to recognize them and think of them as familiar persons, something akin to religious relatives.

And the image of Jesus, always solemn and always beautiful in a special way, made it possible for me to have an idea of his continuous, living presence in the church. Jesus and the saints became, through their icons, not just historical figures, but persons with whom I could relate and to whom I could pray.

It is interesting that the passion of the defenders of icons in the eighth and ninth centuries seemed to flow from a similar personal connection to the icons. The imperial edicts that suppressed the use of icons would have appeared to be nothing less than heartless, blasphemous oppression by a cruel government. Yet one particular symbol remained in favor during this period and was consistently used to replace icons in public places: the depiction of the cross. The cross, technically speaking, still fell under the biblical prohibition against making images of "anything that is in heaven above, or that is in the earth beneath, or that is in the water under the earth." The same commandment insists that "you shall not bow down to them." Nevertheless, the symbol of the cross grew to acceptance as a military symbol and as a symbol of the Christian Empire—as close to modern national symbols and flags as possible.

There is, however, a semiotic difference between the *representation* of the True Cross, which is prohibited under the

Mosaic commandment, and the *symbol* of the cross that is not connected to a particular cross, but rather points to the death of Jesus. In this way, then, the image of the cross would have been less offensive to iconoclasts than icons of Christ, because the symbol of the cross was not suspect in an attempt to represent the divine nature—which was scandal for the iconoclasts.

At any rate, the image of the cross was never questioned by the iconoclasts and the image was widely promoted in the place of icons. All churches from the iconoclastic era feature a great cross in the apse, where earlier churches usually have an eschatological image of Jesus and later churches have an image of Mary as the Queen of Heaven (Platytera).

One possible understanding of this approach is that the iconoclastic faction tried to alleviate doubts aimed at their own piety by stressing the symbol that everyone respected. If this were the case, there is no reason that this change from the sign of the forehead to the large sign of the cross over the body would not be imitated by the iconophiles. Why? Iconophiles had no animosity towards the symbol of the cross, and would perhaps like to show that they were as appreciative of the symbol that identified Christianity more readily than any other, as the iconoclasts were.

That such an established custom may have originated from a heretical group sounds odd. Yet nothing was heretical, as far as anyone could see, about the large sign of the cross. And since this possibility of iconoclastic influence fits the framework and is consistent with the timeframe of the transition of this view of the cross, it should be considered seriously.

Nevertheless, wherever, whenever, or however the practice originated, all Christians, heretic and orthodox, Eastern and Western, embraced it readily.

The next change the sign of the cross underwent had to do with the number of fingers with which it was performed. For several centuries the sign was formed by the motion of two fingers. Yet in later centuries the sign was made by tracing three extended fingers (the thumb, the index and the middle finger), with the remaining two fingers folded against the palm. This began to be the norm in the West, and is still the gesture practiced by most Eastern Christians.

It is difficult to trace the history of when the three-finger sign replaced the two-finger sign. Russian Old Believers, a sect that became schismatic in the seventeenth century, still refuse to use the three-finger sign, practicing that which was customary in the Russian Church before the seventeenth century and which, in turn, was common practice in Byzantium in the tenth century.

By the middle of the ninth century, the emergence of the three-finger sign is already described in the instructions of Pope Leo IV to his clergy: "Sign the chalice and the host with a proper cross . . . with two fingers outstretched and the thumb hidden within them, by which the Trinity is symbolized. Take heed to make this sign rightly."[17] Leo IV in this account, interestingly, witnesses the transition from the two-finger to the three-finger sign. If we create a visual of the hand as he describes it, looking from the side of the palm, we observe the thumb joining the index and the middle finger. Since the thumb is "hidden" and the other two fingers "outstretched" according to the text, if we look at the hand from the other side, we only observe two fingers. This "hidden" positioning of the thumb is the easiest way to perform the sign showing only two fingers. In this way it is possible that the older sign of the two fingers was performed in the way described by Leo IV, in an adaptation of the symbolism of the sign of the cross to refer to the Trinity.

The theology of the Holy Trinity arose as an issue in the ninth century, shortly after the time of Leo IV. The dispute between East and West focused on the addition of the word *filioque* (and from the Son), pertaining to the procession of the Holy Spirit. This dispute remains open to this day. The East, adhering to the Gospel of John's text "the Spirit of truth which proceeds from the Father" and to the text of the Nicene Creed as it had been defined by the first two Ecumenical Councils, and also following the theological view according to which the Father is the source of divinity within the Trinity, maintained that the Holy Spirit proceeded from the Father alone. The West modified the Creed by adding the word *filioque to it*. This first happened in the fifth century in Spain, because the local church had to convince a large number of Arians who were returning to the orthodox church, that the divinity of Jesus was not lesser, or different, from the divinity of the Father.

In addition, whereas the original Greek text of the Creed uses a word (εκπορευεται) that suggests not only procession but also source, the Latin translation used a word (*procedit*) that does not necessarily specify the source of the Holy Spirit, and therefore Latin theologians saw nothing wrong with acknowledging the role of the Son in the procession of the Holy Spirit. In addition to the theological differences, the Eastern church took offense at the addition of a word to the Creed, without proper discussion and without the agreement and approval of an Ecumenical Council—something that the modern community of Churches has also pointed to. Nevertheless, although the theological views that allowed for the addition of the *filioque* to the Creed were accepted in the West, Rome itself added it only in the eleventh century.

At any rate, the issue of the *filioque* was grouped with several other issues of varying importance and political import that increasingly separated the Greek and the Latin Churches. The issue of the *filioque* however, defined the theological field of their antagonism. This may seem distant from us, and the arguments of the two sides may sound like inconsequential opposition about a single word, but the world has not really changed very much since then. I remember that only a few years ago, when I was living in Canada, people had to vote on whether Quebec could be recognized as a "distinct" society. They narrowly avoided a political split, because the inclusion of this single word to the Constitution had political, social, and cultural repercussions that could not be easily understood by someone who did not live the debate from the inside. A word that may define the nature of the Trinity could certainly command more passion, especially in the Middle Ages.

So, as the East and the West were arguing about the theology of the nature of the relationship of the three persons of the

Holy Trinity, both sides decided to make the symbol of the Trinity more evident within the making of the sign of the cross. As a symbol of the crucifixion or as the initials of Christ, the sign was made early on in association only with Jesus Christ, the second person of the Holy Trinity.

The existing evidence, sparse as it is, suggests that the use of the two fingers was widely accepted in the East and the West. From Pope Leo IV's directive, the positioning of the thumb as he directs his clergy to perform the sign, comes from what he considers the traditional, reasonable, and accepted way.

We also know that the change from the relatively ambiguous sign that Leo IV describes to the clearly defined sign with three equally extended fingers, was completely accomplished within a few centuries, at least in the West. A detailed description of the sign from the early thirteenth century corresponds perfectly with the way Eastern Christians still perform the sign, as Pope Innocent III explains how the sign of the cross should be properly traced:

> The sign of the Cross is made with three fingers, because the signing is done together with the invocation of the Trinity. This is how it is done: from above to below, and from the right to the left, because Christ descended from the heavens to the earth, and from the Jews (right) He passed to the Gentiles (left).
>
> Others, however, make the sign of the cross from the left to the right, because from misery (left) we must cross over to glory (right), just as Christ crossed over from death to life, and from Hades to Paradise. [Some

priests] do it this way so that they and the people will be signing themselves in the same way. You can easily verify this—picture the priest facing the people for the blessing—when we make the sign of the cross over the people, it is from left to right.[18]

Tracing the transition of the practice of the sign of the cross in the East is difficult. The Russians continued to use only two fingers until the seventeenth century, when patriarch Nikon instituted a series of liturgical changes aimed to make Russian practices consistent with contemporary Greek practices. The people who did not accept these changes broke off from the Russian Church and were known as "Old Believers." To this day, they perform the sign of the cross with two fingers.

The transition in Greece occurred more quietly. Strangely, one of the sources that archpriest Avvakum (one of the leaders of the Old Believers) invokes to defend the practice of the two fingers, is Maximos the Greek, who lived a century earlier. Yet Maximos, who wrote much of his work when in Russia, may simply have been referring to the existing practice of the Russians, which had, no doubt, ancient roots. Maximos may have left out commenting on the sign of the three fingers, unfamiliar to Russians. He would not have been a fair indicator that the two-fingered sign of the cross was still performed in Greece in the fifteenth century.

Still, the Old Believers found support for their views in the Council of the Hundred Chapters, often referred to as "Stoglav" (meaning "one hundred chapters"). The Stoglav consists of answers to a hundred questions posed to the Holy Synod of the Russian Church by Czar Ivan IV "the Terrible" in 1551. According to chapter 31,

> The sign of the cross must be made according to the rules, in the form of a cross; and the right hand, that is, the dextral hand, must be used in crossing oneself, with the thumb and the two lower fingers joined together, and the extended index finger joined to the middle finger, slightly bent; thus should prelates and priests give their blessing and thus should men cross themselves. It befits all Orthodox Christians to hold their hand thus, and to make the sign of the cross upon their face with two fingers, and to bow, as was mentioned before. If anyone should fail to give his blessing with two fingers, as Christ did, or should fail to make the sign of the cross with two fingers, may he be accursed.

This quote reflects the Russian Church of the sixteenth and seventeenth centuries, a Church resistant to change. The Stoglav in particular reflected an exceptionally conservative spirituality. For this reason the Stoglav does not fairly indicate the spiritual practices of the entire Orthodox East at that time.

While the practice of the sign of the cross has remained exactly the same in the East in the last few centuries, the practice and understanding underwent one additional change in the West. Pope Innocent III, as we saw earlier in this chapter, had already recorded the change from the right cross to the left cross (from the "right to left" to the "left to right"). Still, in both cases he witnessed to the use of three extended fingers.

What used to be the exception regarding the horizontal directional placement of the sign, soon became the rule in the West: All subsequent descriptions as to performing the sign of the cross on the horizontal band agree. The horizontal stretch is to be marked by the fingers from the left to the right shoulder. This identical direction is also found in the Egyptian Church, which offers the same interpretation as the West referencing the Second Coming and petitioning that the faithful not be placed on the left of Christ with the sinners, but on his right, with the righteous. Whether this change in the Egyptian Church occurred as a result of Western influence or took place independently as an adaptation of the large cross made in earlier centuries remains unclear.

The West, however, introduced an additional change, applied after the decision of the three-finger placement of the left-to-right horizontal bar. The sign of the three fingers gave way to the new sign of the open hand, or five fingers outstretched, with which most Western Christians are familiar today.

The change to the open hand likely reflects or rather imitates the blessing of the priest, which in the West is performed similarly, with the entire hand. It is strange, then, that the East maintained the traditional three-finger gesture for the sign of the cross, while the faithful accept the blessing of the priest with a different sign, the sign of the name of Jesus

Christ—which in the Roman Catholic Church can only used by the Pope.[19]

The connection between the sign of blessing and the sign of the cross has always been known. At least this connection has been implied in the East for a long time, even when the two signs were not performed in the same way. In certain cases in the West the sign of the cross was adapted by populations that were not traditionally Christian, so that the connection between the sign of blessing and the sign of the cross would be evident. Although the sign with the open hand emerged as a self-administered blessing, the symbolism of the five wounds of Jesus was later added as an interpretation for it. Yet it is unlikely that the earlier, strong symbolism of the Trinity was replaced—for symbolic reasons—by the symbolism of the five wounds. The more reasonable explanation is that the symbolism of the five wounds came to be applied later to what was already an established practice, when the debate of the Trinitarian symbolism was forgotten.

This interpretation issue does not apply only to the question of the open hand used in signing. There is a particular difficulty with symbols that are practiced over a long time. Sometimes a practice emerges for practical reasons, and only subsequently is a symbolism attached to it. At other times a symbol changes for various reasons, and its original meaning is forgotten, to be replaced by a new one, which is based on the new form of the symbol (although it is also possible for a symbol to evolve as the result of a new way of seeing its significance). This sometimes results in a reading that is not anticipated or intended by those who practiced that symbolic act in the first place.

Many rituals and symbols have been changed for very simple, practical reasons that had little to do with the theological or philosophical content that was subsequently attached to them.

The medieval mind worked in this way. Little interest was placed on the historical development of an idea or a ritual. What mattered was implied by the symbol itself as seen through the prism of the accepted knowledge of the time it was being examined. The same could be applied to earlier time periods. For example, the early Fathers had no difficulty in identifying the symbol of the cross of Christ in the image of Moses parting the Red Sea. Symbols had a life of their own, as it were. This is why people in the Middle Ages were meticulous about the symbols they used.

To present an extreme example of this, let's return to Maximos the Greek. When he witnessed Muslims raising one finger in prayer, he concluded that in this action, Muslims profess the Holy Trinity, even if they do not realize it: "Why do you not raise the thumb instead of the index finger?" he wrote. "Clearly it is because the thumb has only two joints and thus it does not serve to explain the three eternal hypostases. The index finger has three joints and as each joint of the finger in the aggregate structure is called finger but not three fingers, yet all three joints are one finger."[20]

In the East in later times, the connection between the priestly gesture of blessing and the sign of the cross weakened, something that may have to do with the use of the three-finger sign, or possibly the decline of Orthodox theology during the Ottoman occupation. In the eighteenth century Kosmas Aitolos's fifth teaching on the significance of the cross (a long passage mentioned later in this book) touches on many aspects of the sign of the cross, but it does not occur to him to connect it to the priestly blessing. Nevertheless, it was the custom in his time, in earlier times and still today, for lay people to trace the sign of the cross over objects or persons in a form of lay blessing. In the dark times of the Ottoman occupation when Kosmas lived, the connection between the priestly blessing and the sign of the cross was not very clear, and that fact may explain this custom among lay people. Whereas the first was seen as a blessing of sacramental weight, the sign of the cross was, as we see in the teaching of Kosmas, a personal expression of prayer.

This examination of the history of the sign of the cross shows us how the sign developed into a symbol, with every detail having meaning. The sign of the cross, on the other hand, was used rather liberally among early Christians. For many centuries there were no instructions as to the correct way to perform the sign. We can imagine early Christians performing it in different ways throughout the world. Although all testimonies from the early church show that signing one's forehead was the rule, according to the occasion, the believer might sign other parts of their body as well, such as the mouth[21] or the heart. Many Greeks still cross only their heart when they do not want to be conspicuous.

Though few writers provided specific details about how the sign was performed, as certain issues gained in importance throughout the life of the church, in the East and in the

West, they were gradually connected with it. The sign of the cross, like many other aspects of liturgical life, acquired further significance and evolved in order to reflect each additional symbolism more clearly.

After the schism between the Greek and the Latin Churches, and the Fourth Crusade, the relations between East and West were often clouded by mistrust. Many of the cultural differences between the two Churches were seen under a suspicious light, and the currently differing ways the sign of the cross is performed in the East and the West were also seen with distrust. Although it is hardly a theological thesis, and most likely no priest or theologian held such views, I remember that the "rumor" circulated in Greece that the open hand gesture of Western Christians suggested the Trinitarianism of the West was flawed, since they believed in the double procession of the Holy Spirit, and their mistake could be seen in the way they performed the sign of the cross—which does not attest to the number three and the Holy Trinity.

Westerners often have similar reactions when witnessing the Eastern practice, which seems to them either unnecessarily archaic, or wrong. It is often the case, unfortunately, that people cling to practices that are known to them and do not appreciate the historical circumstances that played a role in the development of these practices.

In the historical examination of the evolution of the sign of the cross, nothing suggests that at any given time it had been performed in the same way throughout the Christian world. The varying accounts of Cyril of Jerusalem, Leo IV, Peter of

Damascus, John of Damascus, and Innocent III, and all the other sources we examined, show us how the sign of the cross developed from a simple gesture on the forehead to the three- and five-finger large signs currently in use, but there is little to suggest that such transitions occurred everywhere at the same time.

In addition, the information we have bears witness to practices known in certain parts of the world, such as Rome, Damascus, Constantinople, and Russia.

But historically there have also been silent pockets regarding the theology and practice of the sign of the cross. We have no information about the sign among African Christians, Copts, Franks, Spaniards, Irish, Goths, or Britons in their early history.

Nevertheless, despite the relative lack of descriptions, despite the different symbolic meanings occasionally attached to it, the spiritual weight of the sign has always been the same: In texts from Tertullian and Origen to Kosmas Aitolos, it is a blessing, a prayer, a proclamation of the Christian identity, a living mystery, and an acceptance of the role that God has given us.

CHAPTER THREE

The Need for Symbols and Signs

Religious Semiotics

To understand the gesture of the traced cross of blessing, or of the name of Christ, or of the memorialized crucifixion we must enter a discussion as to the meaning of *signs* and *symbols*. Almost every bit of communication between us and the rest of the world involves some sort of implicitly agreed language, a naturally or arbitrarily formed code that we are all familiar with. In most cases it is as inherent to us as our mother tongue or, for those of us who grew up in the church, our codes and language of what we share in church or at church services. *Language* is the most obvious sign code when we think of conscious communication. Yet there is communication of meaning at other levels as well, such as the linens of a priest's garb, or the way we build and organize our houses or our churches, the way we organize our cities, the way we market products and ideas, and the way we codify our religion.

The way we are integrated as a society involves signs, symbols, and codes. Very few of these codes are meant to be secret; rather, these sign codes are generally agreed upon ways to make sense of our own faith, culture, and civilization. We learn them naturally while growing up, with the result that most of our codes are so obvious that we use them without often realizing we use them. Many of these codes are so closely entangled with our thought process, that it is difficult to imagine something such as "pure thought," separated from, say, language. More than that, the way we are introduced to these codes or languages shapes our thought and our personality.

Only many years after my "tutelage" by my grandfather did I discover the wisdom (or uncanny instinct) in the order he used to introduce me to reading, writing, and stories. He gave me the alphabet first, so that I could explore books on my own, but he did not introduce me to religious stories from the beginning. He started with stories from Greek mythology and history, and in this way I learned how to understand a story—even one that would include miracles, wonders, heroes, and gods. Only after some time, when my mind had digested the process of storytelling, did he proceed to stories from the Bible. He taught me how to follow meanings in mythological tales first, and only then he proceeded with stories that were more difficult to understand because they were true. What is more important, however, is that the final step in my religious initiation as it were, was the introduction to the "doing," to the symbolism of gestures, priestly vestments, and rituals.

The wise old man had helped me proceed from theory to practice, from thinking about a religious story to participating in the ritual that celebrated these stories. Assisting him at the altar I felt I was becoming part of an unfolding story, as if I could see what was important in his teaching from the inside, and not just as an idea I had to listen to. Since then I could see that symbolic or ritual action could be a more complete communication code.

The study of signs and symbols such as these is called semiotics (from the Greek word σημεῖον sign). The study of semiotics makes us conscious of the way we use signs and helps us to uncover hidden meanings in signs and symbols.

Signs consist of two parts, the first which is called a *signifier* (the visible part of the sign, such as the letters of a word or the painting of a train on a street sign). The other part is called its *signified*. This is the actual meaning of the word represented by those letters, or the actual train station. This differentiation is important, because it suggests a distance between what is apparent in a sign and what is really meant by that sign. This distance may be even greater in conceptual or religious signs, because it is simple enough to point to the train that is signified in the traffic sign, but it is not as easy to point to the meaning of signs such as a liturgical procession, an iconographic halo, and certainly the sign of the cross. As in the method of my grandfather, religious stories and symbols are better understood after one has digested the alphabet and the ways of storytelling.

A symbol, whether religious or not, is a special kind of sign. It generally corresponds in some way to a tangible or mental missing part. The etymology of the word "symbol" (from the Greek σύμβολον, consisting of συν and βάλλω) points to the ancient practice of breaking a token of recognition in half—such as a ring or a coin—so that the person who carried the half would honor whatever agreement she or he had entered into, when the other half of the token was presented to them. The meaning of the word *symbol* was subsequently extended toward signifying tangible or intangible things. Generally speaking, the symbol is a sign that does not emerge spontaneously, as other signs do, but when there is a conscious need to refer to its signified.

Religious semiotics or religious symbolism is a special category of semiotics. In a religious symbol we see something of the original meaning of the word "symbol." How? The symbol refers to its missing part, much in way that the other half of the token refers to its counterpart.

Some religious symbols were chosen for historical and dramatic reasons that are no longer obvious. Incense, for instance, was originally used in connection with the sacrifice of slaughtered and burned animals that were offered to God or the gods in several ancient cultures. The offensive smell of many animals, which sometimes had to be completely burned, was counteracted by a simultaneous offering of incense. The image of prayer, purification, and offering was connected with the image of incense wafting towards heaven, because it implied the animal sacrifice. There is no memory of animal sacrifice in contemporary Christian services, but the symbolism of prayer and purification through incense has survived.

Some religious symbols such as priestly vestments are associated with a particular feast day of the Church or suggest a place in the liturgical calendar. Orthodox priests, for instance, wear dark purple vestments during Lent, white vestments at Easter, and red (signifying human flesh and the Incarnation) at Christmas.

In symbols such as incense and the priestly vestments, however, the signifier is connected to the signified only in a representational, almost arbitrary way. There is no real correspondence between the symbol and the spiritual world, but they are used so that we may express our spirituality and voice our prayers. Other religious symbols are—whether by nature or by the sacramental grace of God—essentially connected to their invisible counterpart. Such religious symbols do not refer to an absence, but rather imply the presence of something wholly other than we are, intangible, and pervasively present. The Eucharist is such a symbol. Although different Churches understand the presence of Jesus at the Eucharist in different ways, for many of them the Eucharistic bread and wine correspond to the very presence of Jesus Christ.

The most complete religious symbol as a concept, bringing together the spiritual and the material realms, is Christ himself. In his person, Jesus united the divine and the human. The church, as the body of Christ, maintains the connection between the spiritual and the material world in a similar way. Theologically and liturgically the church expresses the union of the spiritual and the material, a union understood through a highly symbolic expression.

To help understand this concept, think of the souls of the departed or of the angels or of the work of the Holy Spirit. These are things we refer to all the time in the church, although normally we do not have direct experiential connection with them. In the language of semiotics in religious symbolism, the *signifiers* are the icons, the candles, the bread and the wine, and even the sign of the cross, while the *signifieds* are a reality of the spiritual realm of the Kingdom of Heaven.

Early on, Jewish tradition forbade all visual representations. Similarly, in the early church we heard the Fathers of the church warn against the use of symbols that might be confused with their signifieds. For instance, there is a danger in representing God in an icon, say, as a venerable old man in the sky, because what we know about God (Father, Creator, all-good, all-knowing) we know only in a relative and compromised way. Describing God using earthly concepts when we have no direct knowledge of God speaks to this danger.

Another way to look at this concept is the language used when a parent tries to explain the concept of death to a child. Often the metaphor of sleep is used. Sleep is something the child can understand, yet later the child realizes how different the two states really are. Until the child makes the distinction between the two, she or he cannot understand the finality of death, the separation of the body and the spirit. If the child is able to realize that death is "like" sleep but not quite the same, it will be easier to move beyond this initial understanding of death as they grow older.

We are not very different from children in our understanding of that which is wholly other than we are. The mystery of God cannot ever be completely grasped, because God exceeds human understanding. While it is necessary for us to use conventional images we relate to in order to have even an elementary understanding of the Almighty, to meld this mystery into images belonging unmistakably to the material world, prohibits us from getting closer to the mystery.

Extremely anthropomorphic symbols—symbols that attribute human characteristics to God—become obstacles that hinder us from reaching the truth about God beyond the symbols. The description of God as the "Ancient of Days" by the Old Testament prophet Daniel, who used expressions such as "his clothing was as white as snow and the hair of his head was white like wool"[22] can be placed within the framework of ecstatic, prophetic vision. But a visual, iconographic depiction of the Father as a white-haired man in the sky, may give us the wrong idea about God and how we may relate to him.

The Fathers of the church sometimes sought to circumvent the problem of the unseen divinity of the Father by arguing that visions of God in the Old Testament were rather visions of Jesus, the second person of the Holy Trinity, even though he had not yet been born as a man.

But beyond the theological and practical question of whether God can be visible in his divinity, our *depiction* of what cannot be seen is dangerous, because it limits our vista of who or what God really is. In this light, the passage in Scripture that warns of the dangers of anthropomorphism is the famous commandment read by Moses in the book of Exodus, but found in the New Testament book of Romans, in the first chapter: "[T]hey changed the glory of the incorruptible God into an image made like corruptible man . . . and worshiped and served the creature rather than the Creator who is blessed forever."(Romans 1:23-24)

The other direction in religious symbolism, is, rather than many images and icons, the complete absence of iconic symbols or abstract religious symbols where the signifier and the signified are only loosely connected. An example would be ancient abstract or geometric art such as the Minoan symbol of the bullhorns or "horns of consecration." This will be mentioned later in some detail, but the bullhorns, unlike a statue of Zeus, would not have been confused as the object of worship. And ancient Cretans distinguished between the bull as a symbol and real bulls, which were not treated as sacred animals. Later Greek art followed a course of gradual humanization, from Minotaurs and Centaurs to ideal representations of Kouroi and Korai, perfectly formed youths and girls. The Judeo-Christian religious tradition could not be anthropomorphized in this way because it held on to the belief of the invisible, omnipotent, omniscient God.

Symbols of Worship

The symbol and the sign of the cross are different.

The sign of the cross is close enough to the theology of Christianity to evoke Christianity at first sight, yet it is distinct enough from any Christian idea of the divine—it is connected for historical reasons with the work of Jesus, but it does not tell us directly anything about the nature of divinity. Nevertheless, the church has inverted the cross's historical meaning as an instrument of torture and death to one of glorification and eternal life. The discovery and the cult of the True Cross, which emerged during the fourth century, did not change this. Although the theology of the Crucifixion, which was virtually perfected in the early Middle Ages, is an integral part of the Christian experience, an outsider who is not aware of the historical and theological significance of the incarnation and the crucifixion of Jesus, and how they reflect the love of God for humanity, could not possibly guess that the God we profess is "Father Almighty, maker of heaven and earth, and all things visible and invisible. . . ."

The importance of the true (or historical) cross of Christ for Christianity is that of an exceptional relic that came in contact directly with the body and the blood of Jesus during his execution, and it is in this way that it is venerated. Yet, the sign and the symbol of the cross as they are used in the church are not necessarily emulations of the relic of the actual cross of Christ, but a somewhat less relic-specific reference to the death of Christ. The relative indifference of the church about the real shape of the actual cross upon which Jesus died, resulted in its several variations (Greek, Latin, Russian, etc.).

The numerous references by the church Fathers to the sign or the symbol of the cross often use the expression "veneration of the type of the cross." This suggests that the prominence of the symbol of the cross is based on its connection with the death and resurrection of Jesus as it could be re-experienced by the church—for this, any cross would do. The "type of the cross" is not an imitation of the historical cross of Christ, but a symbol of a cross experience. The cross experience, in turn, is also an imitation of the original death of Jesus on the cross. The power and veneration of the symbol of the cross flow from the *sacrifice* of Christ, not from the power of the relic of the True Cross.

It is interesting that the cross was the symbol that icono-clasts promoted instead of icons. Though iconoclasts offered several arguments against the depiction of Jesus and the saints in icons, their main reaction was connected to the Old Testament prohibition against images.

A strict understanding of the biblical prohibition would not have allowed veneration of even the image of the cross. But yet the cross did not trouble iconoclasts, possibly because they realized that the symbol of the cross is not a representation of anything "in heaven above, or in the earth beneath, or in the water under the earth," as it reads in the book of Exodus, but rather a symbol of the passion of Christ. The cross was also closely connected with the Chi-Rho symbol, known as the Christogram or Labarum, introduced by Constantine to conquer and fight in this name; this is the X superimposed over the P in Greek, standing for the name of Christ. Since both symbols had been used widely in the Roman army for a long time, they were sanctioned as military symbols.

The question as to which symbols may be venerated and what definition this veneration holds is not simple. On the one hand, the sacramental and symbolic life of the church includes rituals and objects not essentially connected with what they represent. For the church, on the other hand, the relics of the saints, for instance, and even the icons of these saints, share something of the saint's grace. Therefore, when we venerate a holy relic or the icon of a saint, our honor and veneration reach beyond the decomposed body or the wood of the icon. There is little value in the medium of veneration (the materials, the wood, the gold). The Fathers of the church made it clear that the image or the symbol serves only to convey veneration and honor to the depicted saint or to Jesus.

To many Western Christians whose liturgical practices do not include relics and icons, this will appear as a symptom of scandalous idolatry: to fall down in front of an icon, to make the sign of the cross in front of it and kiss it, to cense it (pouring incense on the icon), to give the saint a special day of observance known as a feast day. And yet, when the Seventh Ecumenical Council convened in Constantinople in 787 to discuss the issue of icons, they made clear the distinction between worship or what they called absolute veneration, which is due only to God, and relative veneration and honor, which could be rendered to saints, icons, and relics, without compromising the absolute veneration due to God the Father as the source of divinity.

The cult of saints, relics, and icons does not diminish the worship of God; instead it celebrates the Trinity by honoring people filled with the Holy Spirit who gained a special proximity to God, and by doing so showed the way for the rest of us. In addition, the saints are considered part of the same community of faithful, even after their death. To address them, pray to them, and ask for their intervention to God, can only be understood within the framework of this community, which is sanctified by the presence of the Holy Spirit and the Eucharistic body of Christ.

The symbol of the cross, however, remains distinct for two reasons. Unlike icons of saints, the cross does not correspond to a particular prototype. And veneration of the cross is based on the cross's imagery and how it recollects the passion of Christ.

In studying the symbolism and the veneration of icons, St. John of Damascus defined categories of religious images based on their properties. In the sixth category of images are those venerated because they "arouse the memory of past events."[23] The symbol or sign of the cross falls under this category, and as a result, as an image it ranks relatively low among the images of religious significance, because the cross—any cross—receives veneration because it arouses the memory of the death of Jesus.

On the other hand, the True Cross, reportedly discovered in Jerusalem by St. Helen, the mother of Constantine, receives the veneration that is due to any holy relic, as it came in contact with the body of Jesus during his sacrifice and death. An exceptional relic, indeed, but categorically not different from the holy shroud, the sudarium (the cloth that covered the crucified Christ's face), or the lance, which do not have particular images made after them.

We may surmise, then, that every cross carries exactly the same semiotic significance and weight. This semiotic significance naturally applies to the sign of the cross as well: The effect and the semiotic importance of the sign of the cross have the same effect and significance as a big decorative church cross.

With that semiotic significance also comes veneration of the sign of the cross, as a symbol. An example from the fifteenth century points to this. The priest Gregory Melissenos, sent in a Greek delegation to the West, wrote about his experience entering an Italian church, a church structure different in style from the Greek churches he was familiar with:

When I enter a Latin church, I do not revere any of the [images of] saints that are there because I do not recognize any of them. At the most, I may recognize Christ, but I do not revere him either, since I do not know in what terms he is inscribed. So I make the sign of the Cross and I revere this sign that I have made myself, and not anything that I see there.[24]

Melissenos knew he was entering a church, and although he could not recognize the icons, he knew what they were and why they were placed there. The different iconographic style did not prevent him from recognizing at least the image of Christ, yet still he did not feel comfortable enough to offer the image the veneration due. His was not so much a question of cultural stylistic differences, as it was of uncertainty as to the spiritual intent of the images. In Melissenos's consideration, these images looked too secular, not "iconographic" enough to claim the connection of grace to the actual Christ, and therefore it was not possible to venerate Christ through them.

Pressed to recognize or establish a place of Christian worship in an environment that was foreign to him, Melissenos naturally turned to the sign of the cross as a means of defining the space of worship around him. For Melissenos, the sign of the cross in these circumstances was a substitute for the other symbolic connections between heaven and earth that he would normally expect to see inside a church.

Something was missing in this Latin church, although at that time there was no theological reason for which

Melissenos would not accept it as a valid place of worship, since the Eastern and the Western churches were within grasp of full communion. The problem was not the increasing doctrinal distance between the East and the West, but that the two parts had been estranged for a long period of time, during which both developed different symbolic languages. Melissenos "did not know in what terms Christ was inscribed," an expression revealing his lack of familiarity with Western symbols of the time, mixed with his distrust of the Western symbolism's ability to serve as a strong connection to the sacred.

Melissenos attended the Latin church to pray as one would pray in a consecrated space, but he failed to recognize what made the church sacred. This perplexed attitude represented a liturgical and theological estrangement between the East and the West, which unfortunately became more distanced with time.

Worship practices still vary within all the Christian traditions, and perhaps Melissenos's response reflects this. For those at home in the Orthodox Church, the long liturgies, various liturgical services such as vespers, matins, and memorial services, an exhaustive Lenten cycle, and icons arranged in strict hierarchical order covering church walls, form part of the religious experience. Yet for those non-Eucharistic services practiced by many Protestants, there is little claim to such elaborate liturgy. In this case a selection of readings and hymns, possibly the recitation of a creed, and then a sermon form the focal point. Compared to the liturgies of the Roman Catholic and Orthodox Churches, many Protestant Churches are seen as minimalist. For those who feel these differences sharply, understanding Melissenos's discomfort in a Latin church makes sense.

The issue may not be ethnic or linguistic differences (Greek and Russian culture, for instance do not have much in common, but their religious culture is very similar), even though these differences often cause misunderstandings among Christians. What Melissenos faced was an altogether different *culture of worship*. At the time Melissenos attended the Latin church, Eastern and Western cultures of worship were alienated from each other, their ecclesiastical unity having been formally broken for more than two centuries. Collaboration on the local level was discouraged, and rivalries increased. As a result, the culture of worship in the East developed differently from that in the West.

While many of the practices of the East retain liturgical continuity with the past, even if they result in a practice that may become stagnant or fossilized, Western spirituality focuses on the written word, seeking an original reading of Scripture. For many Christians it is impossible to sense the sacred in an alien Christian culture. In a manner reminiscent of the reaction of Melissenos in the bare Latin church, Western Christians may feel as though they are entering a pagan temple when they find themselves surrounded by the images, the incense, and the symbols of an Orthodox church.

Many Christians exercise their relationship with God, with the church and with each other through ritual tradition. In Eastern Christianity we find liturgical services, sacraments, periods of fasting and feasting, and stylized prayer, icons, candles, and incense. Each symbol and gesture holds various layers of ritual importance.

Some of these layers reflect a liturgical sense of time within the annual cycle of celebration of the events of the life of Jesus and the saints or other feasts of the church. Other levels speak to the sacraments or to a medieval style of worship, or to the decoration or arrangement of the church building.

These layers reflect different types or levels of worship, corresponding to the different ways through which we understand and relate to the world: through intellect (word), hearing (music), smell (incense) and so forth. Within this range of worship expressions, even the body of the faithful consists of a sacred topos, that is, of a field of ritual significance.

In liturgical practices, the body itself is also used as a symbol. A visitor entering a Byzantine church during a service would see the faithful sitting down or standing up, sometimes turned in a specific direction during prayer, sometimes falling down on their knees or falling prostrate on the floor. At certain times, a visitor would see some in the church kissing icons. And what a visitor would observe often is all the faithful making the sign of the cross—crossing themselves—some repeatedly and nervously, others slowly and contemplatively.

These gestures of the body, like the entire system of ritual worship, affect participants in ways that cannot be completely explained in words. How can worship be reduced to a mental exercise? For many Christians worship does not start and stop with reading or hearing the word of God, using the mind to extract moral teachings from it. For many, a certain degree of bodily response or participation from the congregation is included among the worship tradition of various churches. Perhaps the charismatic churches are known for the most lively participation and expression. Congregations in Eastern churches, however, prefer a highly ritualized approach—which includes the gesture of the sign of the cross, for instance—in expressing the sacred in worship. This does not mean that their participation in the liturgy is passive or restrained. What it means is that they follow certain rituals in order to express their spirituality.

How effective are these rituals, and in what way do they affect or express the faithful? Even in everyday life, we understand that *performing* an action (rather than just talking about it or thinking about it) offers a more complete perspective to a situation. Merely *understanding* a foreign liturgical tradition that includes the sensory practice (not exclusively a textual experience) is only a first step toward appreciating the depths of a tradition. The second step in appreciating a liturgical expressive tradition is to perform some of its practices, allowing the faithful to observe their effect from the inside. How can a person understand an action or practice, if one does not assume the point of view of the person performing it?

A few years ago I visited Edmonton in Alberta, Canada, for the first time. While exploring the city, I got lost. Walking in the downtown area, I tried to remember if I had passed through these streets before, and after a long while walking, I wanted to rest, sit down, and figure out what to do. Not seeing a café or a park bench, I decided to sit down on the pavement for a few minutes, something I would not normally consider doing in Toronto, where I lived at the time. This simple act of sitting on the pavement changed my perspective dramatically. In an instant I felt I had descended to the perceptive level of the homeless. It was a hot summer day, and I was wearing just a pair of jeans and a t-shirt. When I sat down I became almost invisible to the passers-by, and if I had a hat in front of me, some of them might have thrown coins in it—but all passers-by were careful to avoid eye contact.

This simple act, which led inadvertently to a sociological experiment, helped me see how actions suggest a new perspective. To bring this point home, that experience can be related to how the participation in, and not the mere observance of, the rituals of the church may offer a clear perspective of these sacred rituals.

The system of signs, gestures, prostrations, and veneration of icons and relics in the church has an impressive scope, a far-reaching vista. It does not always make a lot of sense from the outside, it's true. And while it is possible to talk in length about the symbolism, the origins, and the aesthetics of this sign and gesture system, the person who has never taken part in it will not fully understand and appreciate its power.

But there is more to liturgical practices than a non-verbal communication of theological ideas. The ritual use of the body in liturgical practices is no mere mechanism by which the sense of the sacred or communal contrition or an "atmosphere of holiness" is established. Symbols such as the sign of the cross, which circumscribe, as it were, the body, give us the sense that the spiritual ascent may be something we share with the rest of the congregation, but it is also something for which we are personally responsible. By crossing or "sealing" ourselves, as one traditional expression calls it, we designate our own selves as the locus of a spiritual struggle, a spiritual battle. Such symbols as the sign of the cross remind us that spiritual salvation is a personal, as well as an ecclesial affair. We bear the sign or "seal" of God, reminiscent of the people marked by angels in the battle in the book of Revelation.

The war described in the book of Revelation is not the only kind of spiritual battle with which the "seal of God" is connected. The sign of the cross addresses the individual's spiritual battle, which is fought on many levels of the self, and is successful when the deepest parts of the personality have come to also reflect the spiritual struggle that the cross attests. The desert Fathers were very aware of this. Most of the ascetic literature essentially represents a sophisticated psychological journey into the self, with Jesus as the compass.

Spiritual warfare, as the experience of the desert ascetics shows, is not so much waged against an external enemy as it takes place within the self. The monks of the desert usually named the demons as their enemies, but it is inside their own minds and hearts that they fought them. They often refer to the sign of the cross as one of the most powerful weapons against demons and temptations, but this clearly shows that they had extended the apocalyptic battle inside them. The sign of the cross and its prayer spirituality showed them the way to do so. The desert monks and theologians spoke often about the descent of the mind into the heart, and about working with the self on levels below our conscious knowledge. We can bring this idea closer to contemporary experience with the insight modern psychology provides. We now know that the deeper we probe into the psyche, the less it looks like our conscious, linearly thinking, calculative intellect. Symbols and archetypes become extremely important on this level. The psyche, especially its deeper parts, is structured according to symbolic principles, which cannot always be addressed in the same ways we address our conscious mind. The deeper level of work in the psychological power of a ritual may be more significant than what rational analysis offers.

The importance of ritual is not a matter of interest to analytical psychology only. Despite the psychological power of symbols and rituals, it would be completely wrong to consider them separated from their spiritual content. Religious symbols and rituals are, more than anything else, a way to follow one's faith.

Doing, performing, acting on a matter of faith is more important than treating faith as a question of membership in the correct school of thought. All this connects with what we think faith *is*. In its secular meaning, faith or belief suggest acceptance of a view or idea without proof to substantiate it—something we may do, for instance, when a person who gives us new information has been proven a reliable source in the past. Faith (or creed) is similar, in this way, to the concept of faith (or credit) in the monetary system, where the value of money reflects a widely accepted trust in a bank that issues a banknote or the state that guarantees that note, a "belief" in the existence of the capital of the bank. To maintain this analogy, one of the pillars of the Christian faith consists of the recorded accounts of the Fathers of the church, Scripture, the holy tradition, and the golden chain of the saints, those who have proved trustworthy and reliable witnesses in transmitting the truth of Christ. The expression "holy tradition" reflects exactly that: the transmission of trust in the church from one generation to another.

There is an additional way to look at faith, however, beyond the acceptance of beliefs that cannot be proven. On a more profound level we can think of faith as an existential condition that brings us closer to God in an experiential way. Faith, on this level, is not an answer to a question (such as the question, "Does God exist?"); rather, faith is the establishment of a living relationship with God that renders abstract questions meaningless in the face of living faith. However, a life of faith as an existential condition, if one begins with the question of God's existence, needs to be nourished by an experiential connection with God. This does not mean a solitary, mystical experience. What the desert Fathers called the ascent towards God may not be found only in the life of the ascetic, but also in the life of any person who lives in faith. The sign of the cross, therefore, has the same significance of spiritual introspection for any believer as it did for the desert monks of the fourth century.

The spiritual realm is not experienced in the solitude of the desert only. Ordinary people experience it in community. Although Scripture and the history of the church have shown several saints and prophets in direct personal encounters with God (as direct as an encounter between God and humans could be), the way God meets with most people is often subtle: A life in Christ is a sacramental life. This life radiates to the people with which it is shared. This sharing makes evident the presence of Jesus in the church and makes evident the image of God in all of us.

These liturgical practices form a culture of worship, which is necessary because in the church we do not aim to attain salvation for ourselves only. We do not exist in a vacuum. We see the image of God in each other. We bring ourselves to prayer together. It is not accidental that the prayer given to us by Jesus is in the plural: "Our Father," not "My Father."

The clearest experience of God for Eastern Christians is the reflection of God in the community that is defined by the unity of the Eucharist. The sign of the cross is the symbol that, like a visible mark of baptism, extends this community beyond the walls of the church building. The Christian "identity" and its profession are evident wherever the sign of the cross is performed. In addition to identifying ourselves as soldiers of Christ—whether anticipating the Second Coming of Christ and the "seal" of the book of Revelation, or thinking of the sign of the cross as a way to examine our innermost thoughts—the sign of the cross also helps us recognize each other and helps us recognize the community that shares in the body of Christ, even apart from the Eucharistic liturgy.

The sign of the cross is but one of the symbols used by the church to express the ineffable. The church as a Eucharistic community defines its symbolic expression and forms its culture of worship through a liturgical tradition that consists of rich symbolic language and theology.

Symbolic Theology

In order to appreciate the importance of the symbol and the sign of the cross, it is important to make a short detour and consider the significance of symbolism and symbolic theology in the Christian tradition. Since the first Christian centuries there have been those who have studied liturgical or symbolic theology. Starting in a Jewish and Hellenistic milieu, Christian worship naturally incorporated rituals from the Jewish tradition. In time, distinctly Christian rituals emerged.

For a long time, these liturgical practices were not questioned, perhaps suggesting how closely the form and the expression of Christianity were connected with its content. The earliest commentaries on the liturgy or on Christian symbolism were not composed in order to defend it against criticism, but rather to connect liturgy and symbolism to the intellectual expressions of Christian theological thought.

No real challenge to liturgical theology emerged until the eighth century, when symbolism and the use of icons in the church were attacked by Emperor Constantine V and others who also questioned the sacramental theology of the church. Clearly, these two issues were intrinsically intertwined. Iconoclasts could not accept icons as valid images of Christ, arguing that the only acceptable image of Christ was the Eucharistic body. Those who defended icons, whose argument eventually won, said that the Eucharistic body was not an image of Christ, but rather the *actual body* of Christ, while icons were *images* of Christ. Clearly, the issue came down to symbolism.

One writer, living in the fifth or sixth century, created some of the earliest and most widely respected works on liturgical and symbolical theology. Essentially he laid the foundations of symbolic theology, and his work is still intriguing today. Strangely, for a person of his long-lasting influence, his real identity is unknown to us. He wrote under the pen name of Dionysius the Areopagite, after a Greek judge mentioned in the book of the Acts of the Apostles. To distinguish this writer from the real Dionysius the Areopagite, he is now usually referred to as pseudo-Dionysius the Areopagite (although several people understandably object to the use of the word "pseudo" for someone who although remains unknown to us has contributed enormously to the tradition of the church).

Among the ideas in pseudo-Dionysius' treatises are his statements about the spiritual world and the angels. He describes the invisible world as a celestial hierarchy of angels that convey the light of God throughout creation. He also writes that we may approach God through the hierarchy of the church and through the sacraments. Extremely influential in the churches of the East and the West, pseudo-Dionysius gave text to much of what we believe and practice in liturgical services. The way we see the sacraments of the church is shaped by his work. One of the central themes of his writings is how sacraments and the church help us picture the spiritual world, as much as that this is possible, and how they help us to ascend towards God.

Again, expressed in contemporary terms, pseudo-Dionysius and other theologians who followed in his path suggest that having a cognitive understanding of God and the invisible realm is impossible for us. Even so, the symbols and the rituals of the church have an effect on us, at levels deeper than the conscious mind. The symbols and rituals turn our soul toward God and invite his grace and the operation of the Holy Spirit. This certainly applies to the symbol and the sign of the cross, which expresses a joyous and triumphant experience of God.

This "turn of the soul toward God" is very different from what today psychologists would call auto-suggestion. Even the monks of the desert and theologians of pseudo-Dionysius' time warned against easily attainable visions or false impressions. They worked diligently to discern between false or satanically induced impressions of spiritual progress, and the actual visitation of the Holy Spirit or a true vision or illumination.

Pseudo-Dionysius spoke of this lifelong quest as a threefold process of ascent. This process consists of stages of purifying the soul, of spiritual illumination, and finally of unification with God beyond all rational explanations. Nevertheless, there is nothing "magical" in the sacraments or the rituals that pseudo-Dionysius writes about, nothing that can bring about a supernatural effect without the participation of the Holy Spirit and without a corresponding "movement of the soul," to use the patristic expression. Even the sacraments in which the Holy Spirit is present, such as baptism or the Eucharist, are not able to bring about a change in someone's life without the active participation of the faithful who receive the sacrament.

Both asceticism (in some form) and the grace of God were seen as necessary for the ascent of the soul. There was no doubt in the minds of Byzantine theologians that in the entire process of ascent, God and humans work together, from the beginning to the end: The expression they used, which reflects this concept accurately, is *synergeia*, cooperation between God and humanity.

In the ascetic ascent of the soul towards God, the soul and the mind encounter realities that do not resemble anything from the material realm. The rituals and symbols of the church are not so much meant to be taken as approximations or visual translations of the invisible world; rather, the rituals and symbols help us establish or strengthen our rapport with the invisible world.

Iconography represents the invisible. Icons seek to symbolize rather than to depict. They seek to present an image from the perspective of God, not to portray our recollection or visualization of the image of a saint. This is why saints who have died a martyr's death are never represented in icons with severed heads or hands, but are depicted as God sees them in his Kingdom: spiritually perfect.

There are photographs of some modern saints, but although they capture the physical likeness of saints accurately, they are not "precise" in the iconographic sense. Photographs depict these saints as they were in this life, not in their present triumphant state in the glory of God.

Iconography melds eternal time, or time as God views it, with the here and now, giving relatively little weight to historical time. This eternal time perspective is also true for the entire art and liturgy of the church. Our liturgical actions position us, symbolically, outside chronological time and into God's time.

Liturgical worship consists of a multitude of activities that involve rituals, sounds, images, vestments, hymns, words, smells, positions, and gestures, which simulate an experience of heaven based on what we have come to know—beyond the secular meaning of knowledge—regarding the invisible world. Liturgical symbols help us pray to God, turn our attention to him, and receive his blessings, either privately or within the community of the faithful.

It is in this context of liturgical symbols that we see the history and framework of the sign of the cross, even if the gesture is not always performed in a communal liturgical environment. Worship is a canvas where every constituent element is important in its own right. In order to appreciate the liturgical significance of the sign of the cross, let us compare it to another gesture of worship.

"Let the lifting up my hands be as an evening sacrifice…"

I remember when I visited the Minoan palace in Knossos, Crete, for the first time many years ago. Like every other tourist I was extremely impressed by the ubiquitous symbol of the bullhorns, commonly referred to in archeological and historical bibliography as the symbol of the "horns of consecration." This symbol, which consists of a horizontal base and two almost vertical blocks at each end of the base at a slightly obtuse angle, can be seen in vases, in statues, in multiple representations in buildings, and in almost anything that claims a "Minoan" identity.

The symbol of the horns of consecration is believed to be connected, on a basic level, with ancient Cretans' fascination with the power and the might of the bull. These horns may be seen in representations of ταυροκαθάψια (bullfights), as well as in other representations of bulls. They are also seen in symbols of mythology connected to Crete (especially the myth of Zeus, Pasiphae, and the Minotaur). In addition, some suggest that the particular angle of the bullhorns reproduces the view of Mt. Youktas, south of Heraklio. The sacramental use of the horns of consecration, however, shows that it is more than a national symbol or mythological symbol. In addition to the religious significance of the bull in the Minoan civilization, other Near Eastern cultures around the same time held a close comparison to the symbol of the horns, revealing an interesting overarching element: The gesture of the horns reflects, precisely, a traditional gesture of prayer with arms lifted upwards. This symbol existed in pre-Christian religions and has survived into and through Christianity and its symbols.[25]

Almost all statuettes of Minoan priests and priestesses represent them with arms lifted up, in the exact obtuse angle that be can seen in the horns of consecration. The resemblance is too exact and too frequent to be coincidental. As I was in the museum of Heraklio looking at all these images of prayer, captured in time, next to several images of the horns of consecration, I could not mistake this universal gesture suggested when ancient Minoans saw that symbol, not of bulls, but of addressing the gods up high, a gesture of prayer. The horns of consecration encapsulated in three simple lines the spirituality of the bull, the practice of prayer, and possibly also the connection of the Cretans with their native land.

The Minoan horns of consecration form an example of how a symbol represented visually, one that also possibly points toward a performed gesture, may represent an entire culture. The symbol may expand to also represent the essential doctrines of a religion. Such expansive symbols can be found in other cultural traditions, although not always with the same powerful overtones. In a similar gesture, Muslims sometimes symbolically "wash their face" in the spirit of God, but since the Islamic tradition does not condone symbolic representation in art, the religious community forms this gesture, reflecting the similarities in, and the same need for, a sacred gesture and sign.

Why do we need signs? Why do we need to express our religiosity in gestures? How do such gestures help us internalize our spirituality? Gestures and signs are essential to spiritual culture since every gesture holds its own spiritual meaning. The ancient gesture of lifting one's arms in prayer indicates an invocation, an appeal, and an attempt to communicate with God up high. It is not a gesture necessarily any more appropriate to Jews and Christians than it is to pagans. In both those traditions "heaven" is either a metaphor for a metaphysical place beyond nature, or, at least for pagans, an approximation of Mt. Olympus. Ancient cosmology was not so much an issue of the mapping of space as it is today, but "heaven" for most religious cultures was formed beyond the places humans understood as limited by physical space. Heaven was formed within a metaphysical framework. As a result the expression "who art in heaven" could be applied to God who is, properly speaking, above and beyond being.

Zeus and the pagan gods also existed beyond boundaries, watching mortals from the top of Mt. Olympus. Therefore, in the pagan tradition addressing the gods up high meant throwing oneself to their gaze.

In ancient cultures the gesture of addressing the heavens with lifted arms was widely understood as a gesture of addressing God. Christian writings reflect this. Early writers, who created commentaries on the Lord's Prayer, insisted that the prayer should be said within the context of arms lifted in this gesture, making the invocation to heaven evident. For Christians, the Lord's Prayer, like most of the prayers of the church, is addressed to the first person of the Holy Trinity— the Father. And lifting up our hands is a suitable gesture of invocation to the Father "who is in heaven."

The Inward Sign

The gesture of the sign of the cross, however, holds a completely different meaning. Throughout its history the sign of the cross has been seen as a mark of Christian identity. From this perspective it is performed so that the sign may be seen by others. This was the case especially in earlier Christian centuries, as well as during times when Christianity became threatened.

According to the sign's other meaning, which has become more prominent in the last twelve centuries, the gesture of the cross is also a self-blessing, a gesture that imitates and reflects the sacramental blessing of the priest.

As both interpretations suggest, it is not directed towards God—unlike the gesture of the outstretched arms. In the first case, as the mark of Christian identity, it is directed at someone else. And in the second case, as a gesture of blessing, the sign is turned toward the self. In both cases, since it is traced over the body, its conceptual start is the most easily graspable sense of the self, which is the body. Where the gesture of the outstretched arms formed an invocation, the inward direction of the sign of the cross creates a gesture of profession of and acceptance of the faith. Both the sign of the cross and the gesture of the outstretched arms signify prayer, but the direction, and therefore the meaning of the prayer formed by the gesture, is different in each case.

Lifting the hands is something we do when we address God in heaven. This form of address works similarly to the way we communicate among ourselves: We speak, and our words are sent, offered toward and heard by the other person. Tracing the sign of the cross over one's body is different. We gesture the sign of the cross when we invite God to talk to us, to accept and clean our body and our entire being, so that our body becomes a temple for God to dwell in. This kind of prayer is more contemplative in nature. It starts with the self and is directed towards God in a kind of inside-out space; our prayer is directed to God in heaven through an inward journey.

Like most religious symbols, the sign of the cross has several layers of meaning. The first and most obvious meaning is Jesus' sacrifice on the cross. Crossing ourselves is an act of acceptance of Jesus' sacrifice on the cross, and also a cross we symbolically take unto ourselves as a symbolic enactment of Jesus' words in the Gospel of Matthew: "If any man will come after me, let him deny himself, and take up his cross, and follow me."[26]

Vast literature has been devoted to the inspiration of the cross, commenting on the cross's ability to sustain in times of difficulty, or noting the pain that Jesus endured on the cross. Still, pain, endurance, and suffering are not the main focus of the way of the cross. Jesus makes this evident by connecting the cross to the denial of the self in the passage from Matthew's Gospel. Rather than death, the way of the cross is submission of the self to the will of God. St. Paul also points to this when he writes to the Galatians, "I have been crucified with Christ and I no longer live, but Christ lives in me."[27]

Inward spirituality is a difficult chapter in the history of corporate worship. Properly speaking, there is no such thing as private prayer in the tradition of the church. Individuals in the church are part of a larger body: No focus is meant to be made in prayer for one's private salvation; no claim is meant to be made to having attained a higher level of "spirituality" than anyone else. The spiritual ascent "of the one to the One" was a pagan ideal, to which Christianity was firmly opposed. In that sense, inward spirituality, or the contemplative withdrawal into the self, is meaningful only if it is still connected to collective prayer, and if the person who prays privately does so while in a connection of love and community with the rest of the church.

In this same way, the sign of the cross starts from the self, but it describes an inward journey that is shared by the entire church and leads back to the church. The way of the cross is not a pursuit for a personal, individual spiritual merit, but an offering of the self to God. The deeper the journey into the self, the more complete is the offering of the self to God. This spiritual analytical journey into the self is practiced to varying degrees by all Christians, though the monks of the desert have lived in the practice of this journey. It is no surprise then, that monasticism is often thought of as the way of the cross.

Monasticism: The Way of the Cross

Although the acceptance of and submission to the will of God is connected to the cross of Christ in the New Testament Gospels and Epistles, it was only later, in the fourth century, that the cross gained momentum as a symbol, as well as an archetype for the life of the Christian. The monastic movement and the desert Fathers inherited the "line of fire" coming after and taking the place of the martyrs whose crowning was a direct imitation of the crucifixion of Jesus. The martyrs faced organized persecution by the Roman Empire, and their challenge was placed before them. For the most part, the challenge had to do with a confession of the Christian faith. The ones among them who were condemned to death were called the "confessors" by others who were with them in prison, as they awaited execution. At that time the highest status in the church was given to martyrs, and they became saints by this martyrdom.

Martyrs and confessors lived and died imitating Christ, and Jesus' death on the cross summed up the Christian ideals of the time, where the church looked to the authority of the confessors in spiritual, doctrinal, and ecclesiastical matters. And though it is difficult to say whether Christians of that era performed the sign of the cross or to know how exactly they gestured the cross, their way of life was based on the imitation of the cross and the sacrifice of Christ in a real and tangible way.

When the church came through the time of persecution, the course of Christianity changed. While it is true that desert ascetics and other predecessors of monastics existed in the first few centuries after Christ, only after Christianity became socially acceptable (and soon, the official religion) did monastic life itself become viewed as a mainstream archetype for Christians.

Two who influenced the direction of ascetic and monastic life were St. Anthony the Great and St. Athanasius of Alexandria. Anthony, considered by many to be the Father of monasticism (known also as the "professor of the desert") left the world to become a religious ascetic in the year 270, forty years before the signing of the Edict of Mediolanum that allowed the church to come out of the catacombs. When he emerged from the desert much later, he was surprised to learn that the emperor was Christian.

And the man to whom we owe our knowledge of St. Anthony, and who also put his own life forth as an archetype of monasticism, Athanasius, was the bishop of Alexandria. He died in 373, only a few years before the Second Ecumenical Council in Constantinople, well after Christianity had become the dominant religion in the Roman Empire. The spirituality of the two men precisely reflects the turning point between the age of the martyrs and the age of the monks.

Athanasius was one of the most famous personalities of his time, a respected bishop who fought heresy. He is regarded as one of the theologians who formulated some of the early and basic doctrines of the church. An ascetic renowned for his holiness and his spiritual struggles, Anthony would have been unknown to us if the respected bishop Athanasius had not written his biography. The eminent theologian saw in Anthony a new model of sanctity, necessary to the changing times. The way and the weight of the cross were ready to be carried on new shoulders. Anthony, the first in a long line of monks that continues uninterrupted to this day, was one who lived the life of the cross in a different way.

The struggle of monks was different from that of the martyrs, even if both developed along similar lines of self-sacrifice. The people who were ready to give their life for Christ were no longer thrown to the lions. Martyrs and confessors were becoming a thing of the past. The imitation of Christ and the ideal of the Crucifixion had to change with the changing times. Many Christians felt they would like to do more toward spiritual advancement and found themselves in the position of the rich young man who asked Jesus how to achieve eternal life, and what was needed beyond obeying the commandments. The answer Jesus gave is recorded in the Gospel of Matthew: "If you want to be perfect, go, sell what you have and give to the poor, and you will have treasures in heaven; and come, follow me."[28] Anthony, who heard this passage in church when he was a rich young man, followed the command immediately, and to the letter. He left the world and his riches for the Egyptian desert. Other people followed his example, and soon, as the writers of that time tell us, the desert was as populated by as many ascetics as a large city. A similar movement took place in Palestine, and soon monasticism spread to the entire known world.

Monasticism quickly became the new ideal of the perfect Christian life, replacing the Christian ideal of martyrs. Although the underlying concept of self-sacrifice in imitation of Christ was the same, the difference was that the imitation of Christ took an inward turn, and it came to mean the submission of the self, the struggle against the passions of the soul. The new enemy was to be found in the demons who wandered in the wilderness, and not in the soldiers of the pagan Emperor. The ideal of sacrificing the self and the symbolism of the cross, became less literal and more spiritual. The church responded to the new model of spirituality, and quickly it became customary to choose monks to govern the church, becoming the new voices of spiritual authority. Bishops were chosen from the ranks of monks, and this way of choosing bishops eventually became the standard.

It has to be noted here that the way of the monk is not that of individual salvation. The image of flight into the desert may appear to contradict the sense of togetherness that we see in the church, especially after we established that prayer and spiritual struggle are not a private, individual affair. Strange as it may appear to us, monks were not praying for their individual salvation, but on behalf of the entire church. Sometimes they saw themselves as border guards who fought demons so that they would not torture the rest of the church. In this way they often explored the limits of spiritual ascent and passed their experience to the body of the church. Even in our times, there are monks who pray for the salvation of humankind, and in moments of humility cry "everyone will be saved, except me!" But the normal model for the life of the monk is St. Anthony, who spent fifty years of his life in isolation, and the following fifty years as a monk in the world, assisting everyone else with his counsel and in any other way he could. Monks form a special relationship with the body of the church, in which they join common prayer from their cell.

Already by the fourth century, shortly after the time of Anthony, educated theologians accepted monastic tonsure and went into the desert, or any place of solitude available to them, in order to fight their demons. People such as Evagrius of Pontos and the unknown author of the Makarian homilies developed sophisticated methods for delving into the deepest parts of the self, and crucifying its lurking vices. The valuable insights of people who made prayer their full-time profession showed others that the image of the cross is a way to invite the grace of God. The Makarian homilies tell us so directly: In his spiritual fight against the passions, their author saw a luminous cross plunging itself deep into the inner man, after which the grace of God quieted all his parts and his heart.[29] The ascetic here literally invited the sign of the cross into his innermost self. This is not an exception. Ascetic literature is filled with similar images. The early Egyptian desert monks showed the cross's importance for them, when they adopted the mark of the cross on their habits to signify to the world that they lived the life of the cross.

The struggle of the desert monks provided the spiritual background for the emergence of the cross as the most well known Christian symbol; and from the monks, the church propagated it to the rest of the world. The symbol of the cross now took on a wider meaning than the one it had in the age of the martyrs, and the cross quickly became synonymous with Christian identity. The association of the way of the cross with the monastic movement was very important in this regard, but an additional association explains its prevalence: military power and symbolism.

The Emperor Constantine adopted the cross as a military standard in the fourth century. He based his decision on a miraculous vision he had of the luminous cross in mid-air. Years later, his mother, Helen, organized a search for the True Cross of Christ in the Holy Land. According to tradition, the True Cross was found when it evidenced miraculous power. The adoration of the True Cross became a strong movement, especially in Jerusalem. The traveler nun Egeria visited Jerusalem a few years after the discovery of the cross, and described a developed cult complete with processions, public venerations, services, and vigils. She also described a great influx of people coming from all parts of the empire to see and honor the holy relic. During this time, the empire was gradually restructuring its identity, leaving the pagan past behind. The symbol of the cross, present in the Christian tradition from the beginning, became part of the new Christian identity of the Roman Empire, replacing older images of a deified emperor, among others.

No one is certain how the political strain and the religious strains met. Perhaps Constantine saw his army as similar to the ranks of monks. Perhaps Pachomius thought it appropriate to give the desert monks the cross on their cowls as a symbol of spiritual obedience, similar to the obedience of army soldiers. No one is certain. What we do know is that in the fourth century the symbol of the cross was adopted both by the army of the Roman Empire as it became Christianized, and by the monks of the desert, who organized themselves as the army of God.

Although all these factors played a role in the prevalence of the symbol of the cross in the fourth century, the message of the cross was not exclusively for those who lived in monastic vows. The spiritualized message of the cross applied to monastics and laymen equally. The imitation of the crucifixion of Christ was interpreted as the submission of the self and the death of the passions, a struggle for all Christians. Yes, the vocabulary of spiritual ascent was compiled by the desert Fathers, but the sign of the cross was embraced by all. The way of the cross is not measured in self-deprivation, but in the death of the self and the resurrection in Christ for all Christians, not only monastics.

It is relatively easy to visualize the way of the cross within a monastic setting, yet Christianity has always prided itself in the preservation of the tradition, as it is reflected in the totality—the catholicity—of its experience. The truth of the church is not to be found in any distinct, more "spiritual" place than others, but in the combined experience and input of the parish, the monastery, the layman, and the cleric. The words that Greeks and Russians use for "church" (*Ekklesia* and *Sobor*) suggest an assembly and togetherness. And the root of the word *catholic*, which is used not only by the Roman Catholic Church but also by Orthodox and Protestant Churches, points exactly to this totality of the Christian experience. The sign of the cross reflects this catholicity, because it is performed by every member of the church in exactly the same way, and it represents every member of the church in exactly the same way. Monks, bishops, laypeople, and priests cross themselves in the same manner. Unlike symbols such as vestments, and gestures such as the sign of blessing, which are used only by priests and bishops, the sign of the cross is used by everyone, in any setting.

The sign of the cross, from its early forms and throughout the history of the church, has brought together, in a spiritually functional manner, the depth of the journey to the innermost parts of the self alongside communal worship. The sign of the cross helps Christians internalize the messages of the crucifixion and the life of Jesus, making the message personal. At the same time, the sign of the cross connects us to other members of the church. It is a sign as private as it is public, as individual as it is communal. In tracing the sign of the cross over our body, we acknowledge our connection to Jesus, to the church and the community of saints, and to the Kingdom of Heaven that resides inside us.

CHAPTER FOUR

A Prayer to Christ

K osmas Aitolos, an eighteenth-century monk of Mt. Athos, traveled in Ottoman-occupied Greece seeking to inspire subdued Christians with his fervent sermons. He founded more than a hundred schools and churches and was recognized by the Greek Church as an *isapostolos* (equal to the apostles) for his work. One characteristic of his missionary work was that wherever he went he planted a simple wooden cross with its base in the ground. The cross was his missionary signature and a public call for the renewal of the Christian ethos and consciousness. In 1779 Kosmas died the death of a martyr, but his work and those crosses are still remembered. Many people continue to read his sermons and are touched by their simplicity and piety. In his fifth teaching he dedicates a long passage to the spirituality of the sign of the cross:

Listen dear Christians, how the sign of the cross should be performed and what is its significance. The Holy Gospel tells us that the Holy Trinity, God, is glorified in heaven more than the angels. What do you have to do? You bring together the three fingers of your right hand and, since you cannot ascend to heaven to venerate God, you place your hand on your head, because your head is round and signifies heaven, while you say: "as you angels glorify the Holy Trinity in heaven, so do I, an unworthy servant, I glorify and venerate the Holy Trinity. And as these fingers are three—together and separate—so is the Holy Trinity, God, three persons and only one God." You take your hand off your head and you bring it to your belly while you say: "I adore and venerate you my Lord, because you accepted to be incarnated in the womb of the Theotokos for our sins." Then you place it on your right shoulder and you say: "I beseech you, my God, to forgive me and to put me on your right, with the righteous." Placing your hand on your left shoulder you say: "I beg you, my Lord, do not put me on your left with the sinners." Then, falling to the earth you say: "I glorify you, my God, I venerate and adore you, and as you were put into the grave, so will I." And when you get up you signify the Resurrection and you say: "I glorify you my Lord, I venerate and adore you, because you were raised from the dead to give us the eternal life." This is what the holy sign of the cross means.

Kosmas's sermon brings forth one particular aspect of the sign of the cross: the sign of the cross as a prayer. This should not appear strange to us, as the idea is not new. Throughout its history the sign of the cross was always connected with prayer. It was always accompanied by prayer, even if silently, and it inspired meditative prayer.

Yet, the prayer of the sign of the cross is no simple act, and may not directly address Christ. This is true elsewhere in prayer, as well. In the liturgy, for instance, we address the

Father, with the exception of very few prayers and hymns specifically directed to Jesus, even though the formative presence of Jesus in the liturgy is beyond doubt. The liturgy makes continuous references to the drama of Christ, the Incarnation, the Passion, the Resurrection, and the Second Coming. In many ways, the liturgy reenacts Jesus' life, but for the most part these references are meant not as a meditation and prayer *to* Christ, but as prayer *about* Christ. The sign of the cross, similarly, is a form of prayer without words. We know that the sign is closely connected to the life of Jesus, but is it addressed to him? We have learned some of its history and theology, but at this stage one must wonder, keeping in mind the mystery of the sign of the cross: What exactly is this wordless prayer of the cross, and to whom is it addressed? And the sign of the cross is one example of wordless prayer. Are there other wordless prayers in the life of the church?

Levels of Prayer

There are many levels of prayer. Most of us are acquainted with the form of prayer that is a petition, a request to God to grant us the things we desire. This is certainly an aspect of prayer based on the Gospel. St. Paul puts this type of prayer into the larger perspective when he instructs the Philippians in his letter to them, "Do not be anxious about anything, but in everything, by prayer and petition, with thanksgiving, present your requests to God. And the peace of God, which transcends all understanding, will guard your hearts and your minds in Christ Jesus."[30] Petitionary prayer is common in the church. During the liturgy we pray repeatedly for good and seasonable weather, for our well-being, and for the well-being of our loved ones; we even pray for our beloved dead. In other letters, St. Paul encourages Christians to pray for him, and he informs them that he also prays for them.

Other Scripture passages suggest that there are other types of prayer, beyond petition. In St. Paul's famous exhortation, he tells the Thessalonians in his first letter to them to "pray ceaselessly."[31] Other Scripture passages address specific and clear spiritual needs, such as the letter to the Ephesians: "I pray that the God of our Lord Jesus Christ, the Father of glory, may give unto you the spirit of wisdom and revelation in the knowledge of him." (Ephesians 1:17) In the book of Romans, we find a more mystical explanation of prayer: "We do not know what we should pray for as we ought, but the Spirit himself makes intercession for us with groanings which cannot be uttered. Now he who searches the hearts knows what the mind of the Spirit is, because he makes intercession for the saints according to the will of God."[32] The writings of St. Paul provide a wide discussion of prayer in the life of the church. The last passage offers an especially interesting view of prayer in light of the discussion of the significance of the sign of the cross, since this quote from Romans hints at prayer at a level beyond words.

Prayer in the Gospels appears in many of the significant moments in the life of Jesus, such as the Transfiguration, the vigil at Gethsemane, and instances where Jesus prays alone. In these cases, prayer seems to be a manifestation of the connection between Jesus and the Father, and also an example for his followers, who affirm this connection between themselves and God in this way of prayer. In most of the cases we could easily interchange the expression "Jesus prayed" with the expression "Jesus spoke with the Father in heaven," without changing the meaning of the passage.

In the New Testament, no explanation of prayer is usually offered, and rarely is prayer connected to a request. There are two cases where this changes, however: in the difficult prayer in Gethsemane, and when Jesus tells his disciples, recorded in the Gospels of Matthew and Mark, that a certain kind of miracle may be achieved only with "prayer and fasting."[33] The first case, of Jesus' prayer in Gethsemane, nevertheless provides us with a model of submission to the divine will, something that becomes evident in the way Jesus ends his prayer in the Gospel of Luke: "[N]evertheless, not my will, but yours, be done."[34] The second passage from the Gospel of Matthew teaches that prayer and fasting are connected, practices that work together and augment each other.

In Matthew and Luke's Gospels, Jesus gives us, at the request of his disciples, the model prayer known as the Lord's Prayer, present in every service of the church. Only one of the phrases contained in the prayer ("Give us today our daily bread") may be possibly taken as a prayer of supplication, although other parts of the Bible discourage this reading too. In fact, one of the instructions given by Jesus in Matthew's version is, "Your Father knows the things you have need of before you ask him,"[35] suggesting that prayers of supplication are redundant. As for the conclusion of the prayer, "lead us not into temptation, but deliver us from evil," this is not a petition that addresses our own practical needs and desires, but a request for God's assistance in our fight against the desires that may lead us away from God. The Lord's Prayer is the prayer that answers the question for us all: "What can we say to God?"

The church Fathers have contributed to our understanding of this simple prayer given to us directly by Jesus. Among the things the Fathers point to is that this model prayer engages the believer as an act of active and free submission to the glory, the kingdom, and the will of God. The prayer recognizes the dominion of God over both heaven and earth and offers a humble recognition of our sinfulness. The Lord's Prayer also requests God's assistance in the spiritual fight against evil and temptation. This simple prayer reveals very clearly what God expects us to do.

The Lord's Prayer, as well as the few biblical passages just reviewed, suggest that although expressing our requests to God is a valid and recognized aspect of prayer, the presentation of a mere "grocery list" of requests can become a superficial form of prayer. Based on biblical testimonies on prayer, there is more to prayer. As Jesus in the Gospel of Matthew explains, God already knows what we need, before we utter the prayer, before we even realize our own need. In the first letter to the Corinthians, St. Paul discusses prayer, joining prayer "with the spirit" and prayer "with understanding": "If I pray in a tongue, my spirit prays, but my understanding is unfruitful. What is the conclusion then? I will pray with the spirit, and I will also pray with the understanding. I will sing with the spirit, and I will also sing with the understanding."[36] This describes one of the mysteries of prayer: We are called to trust God and place ourselves in his hands, enlisting in prayer every part of our conscious and subconscious self.

This submission and offering of the self has deep roots in Christian theology and worship. Prayer, especially in the East, is connected with a long tradition of spiritual ascent, a means to ascend to God and unite with him. It has to be noted nevertheless, that as the councils and the writings of the fifteenth-century Orthodox Church[37] show, this mystical ascent was sometimes fought in isolation, but was never considered an individual affair outside the collective setting of the church. Prayer, fasting, and meditation were always part of the Christian life, but after the emergence of monasticism these practices evolved into a lifelong spiritual exercise.

Monastic writers such as Evagrius of Pontos, the writer of the Makarian homilies, the Cappadocian Fathers, and countless anonymous men and women dedicated themselves to a life of contemplation in the fourth century, laying the foundations for the church's tradition of prayer.

Practical manuals of prayer were written as instruction to young and more inexperienced monks, manuals still regarded as valuable guides in the spiritual struggle. And while the desert monks followed the solitary way to God, the core spiritual experiences apply to all Christians. Taking their theological vocabulary from the Platonist and Neoplatonist tradition, the ascetics sought to transcend the distance between heaven and earth. The cultivation of the virtues and the fight against the vices, the struggle against the self and the crucifixion of the will are part of the monastic legacy. Eventually, according to this tradition of contemplative prayer, monastics hoped for us to participate in the energies of God, and in this way also to participate in his divinity. It is significant that the entire ascetic and mystical tradition was inextricably connected with prayer as one of the ways to God.

The expression "to participate in the energies of God" refers to the spiritual ascent of the Christian mystics where prayer was sometimes accompanied or affirmed by the experience of Uncreated Light. The key phrase "energies of God" speaks about something somber: On an elementary level, participation in these energies of God suggests allowing God to act through us, recognizing the way God operates in the world, and letting the will of God, after we discern it, guide our own actions or "energies." In this way we ourselves become part of the plan of God and his work in the world. Our will becomes the same as the will of God, and our life becomes an emulation of the life of Jesus, the incarnate God.

It is important to remember that desert monastics kept Christ as their focus in contemplative prayer. There is one short prayer that was used again and again beginning in the fourth century and continuing today, by people who wanted to take prayer from their lips to their mind and to their heart. This prayer consists of naming the name of Jesus and offering a short supplication: "Jesus Christ, Son of God, have mercy on me." This prayer phrase is known as the *Jesus prayer*. Old monks who repeat it in solitude sometimes simplify it even more, praying with only the name "Jesus" on their lips. Fortunately, in recent years, many books about the Jesus prayer and the meditative hesychastic tradition have been published.[38] This simple prayer serves as a way to turn the attention of the person in prayer to Christ. And this is not very different from the way one prays with the sign of the cross.

The fifth teaching of Kosmas Aitolos translates the experience of the sign of the cross into a meditation on the life of Jesus. In fact, the sign of the cross has never been as celebrated as the Jesus prayer, which originated in the fourth century but found itself in the middle of a theological controversy much later. As a matter of fact, most people did not know much about the Jesus prayer and the hesychastic tradition until these practices were challenged in the fourteenth century by a monk who could not appreciate the prayer traditions. His questioning and debate caused a formal sanction of the prayer in a series of church Councils. For centuries, the sign of the cross has been one of the most familiar ways that Christians pray in order to turn their mind to the life, the passion, and the resurrection of Jesus Christ and pray to him, sometimes in silence, and sometimes accompanying the sign by words.

The Sign of the Cross as a Wordless Prayer

How is it possible to compare the sign of the cross to the Jesus prayer, on a practical level? They are both closely connected with Jesus Christ, they both offer an entry point for prayer and meditation on Jesus and his life, and they both offer themselves to the possibility of increasingly deepening levels of meaning, from the remembrance of the historical life of Jesus, to "pure" prayer beyond images and words.

They are different in that the sign of the cross is more integrated in regular activities of the church, whereas the Jesus prayer normally presupposes that we separate ourselves physically from others—although it is not unusual for people who have been practicing the Jesus prayer for a long time to carry it alongside their everyday activities. The sign of the cross was always part of mainstream liturgical practices, private and communal, and as a result it was never associated with one practice, service, or Christian tradition in particular.

While the Jesus prayer can be repeated and can lead into long, meditative sessions, the sign of the cross is not performed or repeated without a specific reason. It is not unusual to see a praying person or the congregation of a church crossing themselves often, sometimes repeatedly, but it is usually an action, a phrase in the liturgy or a word or a prayer that necessitates the sign of the cross. Rather than being a practice that can wedge the mind into a meditative session, it contributes its particular meditative weight to the sum of the tradition of the church. In fact, early Christians in particular insisted on making the sign of the cross at every action, in this way consecrating every part of their lives. This is shown vividly in an account by St. Silouan, who lived in the early twentieth century. He was traveling by train when another passenger in the same car offered him a cigarette. St. Silouan accepted it, thanked the passenger, and asked him to join him in making the sign of the cross before they smoked it—

in the same manner one makes the sign of the cross before a meal. The passenger was puzzled by this and said that it is not usual, or rather it was not proper, to make the sign of the cross before smoking a cigarette. The saint then replied that an action that does not agree with the sign of the cross should not be done at all.[39]

There are many historical readings that discuss the symbolism of the sign of the cross. Along with the teachings of Kosmas Aitolos is the equally famous fifteenth-century account of the Bridgettine Nuns of Sion in the *Myroure of Oure Ladye*:

> And then ye bless you with the sygne of the holy crosse, to chase away the fiend with all his deceytes. For, as Chrysostome sayth, wherever the fiends see the signe of the crosse, they flye away, dreading it as a staffe that they are beaten withall. And in thys blessinge ye beginne with youre hande at the hedde downwarde, and then to the lefte side and byleve that our Lord Jesu Christe came down from the head, that is from the Father into erthe by his holy Incarnation, and from the erthe into the left syde, that is hell, by his bitter Passion, and from thence into his Father's righte syde by his glorious Ascension.[40]

Christ is a Mystery, in the mystical as well as in the sacramental sense of the word, and the more we approach him as such and we delve into the mystery, the more we come closer to God. We cannot say that we understand the mystery or the work of Jesus, but we can ask God to give us a sense of this mystery, which is beyond words.

In the history of the church this has always been done in several levels, starting with the obvious ones: We start with the literal meaning of the Bible, even before we try to identify and interpret its symbolic, metaphoric, and "anagogic" (having a secondary spiritual meaning) layers. The Gospels give us testimony for the work of Jesus in the world. This testimony, according to the church Fathers, is "sufficient" for our salvation. In prayer we also start with remembering and giving thanks for the life of Jesus in this historic past, even as our prayers lead to a union with God in the present moment. In this way, our prayer and our liturgical symbolism are grounded on the life of Jesus.

The historical work of Jesus was accomplished through his incarnation, his crucifixion and his resurrection, and we are called to emulate these in our own lives. The sign of the cross as a gesture of prayer is complex enough to reflect the salvific work of Christ in all its stages. The passage from the fifteenth-century *Myroure of Oure Ladye* sees the Incarnation in the downward movement of the hand from the forehead to the chest, the Passion and Resurrection in the movement from the chest to the left shoulder, and the Ascension in the movement to the right shoulder (as Jesus ascended to the right hand of the Father).

The sign of the cross reminds us, with its suggestive inward direction, that we are internalizing the life of Jesus, his incarnation, passion, and resurrection. But this leads us to the natural question: Many Christians understand patterning their lives after the passion of Christ, as a submission to the divine will, but how do we pattern our lives after Jesus' incarnation and resurrection?

In order to understand the question better, it will help us to look at the context of the historical biblical information within the early church. It may surprise readers to learn that the early church had relatively little interest in the historical aspect of the life of Jesus. Jerusalem, Bethlehem, and Nazareth were relatively unimportant places for Christians in the first few centuries after Christ.

In the church, the liturgical significance of this observation is that the celebration of the events of Jesus' life was not oriented towards the events as historical (at least in the sense we understand "historical" today), but rather toward their significance for the church. The life of Jesus had its focus not in the historical account of the life of an exceptional person, but as the key to eternal salvation.

In addition, the Christian Bible does not end with the ascension of Jesus, but the history of the early church continues with the Acts of the Apostles and the Epistles, integrating the life of the early church with the life of Christ. More important, the gospel and the church were not seen as two different poles of spirituality (as was sometimes the case at points in later centuries). Both were seen as necessary in approaching the ineffable truth of Christ, as they revealed something about each other. The gospel was the product of the church, which exists because of the gospel of Christ. Both were identified with Jesus and his continuing presence on the earth.

The church is the body of Christ on the earth, and the feasts of Christ are feasts of the church. Therefore, all the events in the life of Jesus were seen as events in the life of the church, or at least as events whose meaning was useful so far as they spoke meaningfully about the life of the church. The liturgical life of the church is not a mere commemoration or reenactment, but an active engagement with Christ made possible by the various liturgical symbols. The summation of the life of Jesus in the symbol and the sign of the cross is not meant so much as an act of "taking up" the cross, as it is of "taking the cross inside." The direction of the sign of the cross is inward, which suggests embracing and internalizing the life of Jesus. Nevertheless, this inward direction suggests that, starting with the historical events of the life of Jesus, we live these events here and now, appropriating them outside time and space, as we become one with the timeless Christ.

Our prayer does not stop with historical commemoration; prayer starts with it. Beginning with the gospel, we embark on the ascending journey of prayer, which transforms our lives. Living the life of Christ does not mean, for most people, that we transfer ourselves mentally to Calvary, Jerusalem, and Bethlehem, or transfer ourselves to experience the nails of the cross in the form of the stigmata, but in accepting the living Jesus inside us. We emulate his life as members of his church and his body on the earth, filled with his grace.

The Incarnation

How are we called to emulate the Incarnation of Christ? At Christmas, activity in the media, the marketplace, and most Christian homes reflects an interest in an exchange of good-will and presents. The celebration of the birth of Jesus Christ is a small part of the late-December activities. Even among conscious Christians, the message of the incarnation of Christ is not obvious. The Nativity of Christ is now associated with images of the baby Jesus in a manger, with the veneration of the Magi and the warm breath of the animals in the stable, or in a small hut covered with snow. Apart from visual differences between this scene and the scene of the Nativity as it is pictured in early iconography (which placed the event in a dry, rocky Palestinian cave), the Incarnation, the advent of Christ in the world, is not only about the historical birth of the second person of the Trinity in the body of a human being, but also about the continuous birth of God within the earthly body of Christ—the church. The Incarnation signifies the birth of Christ *inside* all Christians.

The physical birth of Jesus has something in common with Epiphany, with the instance when the Father's voice and the visual manifestation of the Holy Spirit revealed to the world the divinity of Jesus Christ. In fact, Christmas in the ancient church was celebrated together with Jesus' baptism as a celebration of the manifestation of Christ on the earth.

Yet, in historical time, the actual descent of the second person of the Holy Trinity, imperceptible by almost everyone, took place nine months earlier, and was celebrated at the Annunciation of Mary. The Annunciation was seen for a long time as the actual incarnation of the Word, which was accomplished with the Word of God. Mary was exalted and seen as the model of Christians exactly because she gave herself to a life of prayer and acquiesced to the birth of the Word of God inside her. The birth of God inside us, whether referring to the Mother of God or to every Christian, is brought about by the submission of the self to the will of God and a life of prayer.

This is how the meaning of the Incarnation becomes a personal and ecclesiastical event, and how the meaning connects with prayer. The sign of the cross, a gesture of acceptance, shows acceptance of the will of God. The descending movement of the hand from the forehead to the heart is for many Christians, as we have already seen, a reference to the historical descent of the Word on the earth and inside us. As a symbol of prayer the gesture reverberates with Mary's life of prayer in the Temple, and with her offering herself to God. Similarly, signing or crossing our body, we consign it and our entire selves to God as a temple of the Holy Spirit, so that the Word of God may enter us and be born inside us.

Prayer is an act of pure love. Prayer is the fruit of faith that is given selflessly, as one gives oneself to the beloved. And the sign of the cross, with which we start and end our prayer, is the symbol of this love for God and of the longing for his presence and visitation. The sign of the cross is at the same time a blessing of our body and our selves as belonging to the One who created us, and it also symbolizes the sacred birth of the Word, the continuous incarnation of Jesus in his church through us.

The Crucifixion

How are we called to emulate Jesus' Crucifixion? The early Christians who lived in the age of persecutions could answer this question easily: Imitating the Crucifixion was an acceptance of the missionary and apostolic work of the church, an acceptance that almost inevitably led to martyrdom. This view of emulating the Crucifixion, as it was carried by martyrs and confessors who held the highest moral and spiritual authority in the church, continued until the recognition of Christianity as the official religion of the Roman Empire, where the ideals of emulating the Crucifixion changed, as it was no longer connected with a martyr's death.

The crucifixion of Jesus posed a challenge to creating a new model, where the previous ideal of imitating Christ was martyrdom. The new model of crucifixion was based on St. Paul's writings about the death of the old self and new life in Christ. To the Galatians St. Paul wrote, "I have been crucified with Christ; it is no longer I who live, but Christ lives in me; and the life which I now live in the flesh I live by faith in the Son of God, who loved me and gave himself for me."[41] In the book of Romans he stated it another way, "If we have been united together in the likeness of his death, certainly we also shall be in the likeness of his resurrection, knowing this, that our old man was crucified with him, that the body of sin might be done away with, that we should no longer be slaves of sin. For he who has died has been freed from sin."[42]

For St. Paul and the changing church of the fourth century, and continuing on to the church today, the view of the Crucifixion became something else: an event to share with Christ, a continuous process of death and life in Christ. Imitation of Christ and participation in his crucifixion entails setting aside the self through accepting salvation from the weight of sin. It also entails offering ourselves to the will of God, not as a means of pointless servitude, but in freely entering into a relationship with God, even if that relationship incurs suffering. "Why do we suffer?" is one of the recurring questions that the church has tried to answer in every generation, and for this reason this question represents a large part of Christian theology.

Suffering is only one aspect of the imitation of the Crucifixion. The Crucifixion in the early church was seen as having a triumphant character. Carrying one's cross, difficult as it may be, is not meaningful if it is seen only as an act of enduring. Its importance is realized when we learn to discern and recognize the wisdom of God and his actions as they affect our life. The meaning of carrying the cross is not to learn to suffer blindly, but to submit and share in the will of God; it is learning to recognize the providence of God, however painful the crucifixion of our own desires. This process of recognition and acceptance—or "active passivity"—is expressed by the sign of prayer.

The crucifixion of Jesus is, strangely enough, the most ecclesiastical event in his life. Although we may think of the institution of the Eucharist at the Last Supper as the foundation of the Christian church, the Crucifixion is the event that gives meaning to the Eucharist. Jesus referred to his crucifixion in these terms in John's Gospel: "When I am lifted up from the earth, I will draw all people to myself."[43] The sacrifice of Christ was given on behalf of all humanity, and the participation of the Eucharistic community in the body and the blood of Jesus stems from this offering.

The church owes its metaphysical state of grace to the presence in it of Jesus and the Holy Spirit, who unite the faithful into the Eucharistic body of Christ. This body and the Eucharistic community exist because of the mystery of the cross, and the recognition of the mystery and our participation in the mystery of the Crucifixion—our death and renewal in Christ. This is what transforms a gathering of the faithful into a church. The church is not a social institution of this world; it is a heavenly connection, by the way of the cross.

The sign of the cross as a prayer is not a mere request for help and courage for the little personal crosses we may bear in our own life (although this certainly is one of its obvious messages). The sign of the cross signifies our participation in the body of the church. The sign throughout history has been an identifying mark of Christianity, its mystical significance connecting each of us with the larger body of the church and with the Crucified Christ.

The mystical prayer that connects us to the Crucified Christ—by words, by thoughts, by signs or symbols—is not just a prayer of supplication in difficult times, but an action of ascent to the life-saving cross of Christ, an acceptance of the invitation of Jesus to follow him to heaven through the cross. The sign of the cross still maintains the triumphal character the Crucifixion held for early Christians. Performing the sign of the cross in moments of difficulty, but also in moments of celebration and thanksgiving to God, also reflects this use of the sign of the cross as a prayer of glorification.

The Resurrection

Since the beginning of Christianity, there has been no real separation between the event and theology of the Crucifixion and the event and theology of the Resurrection, because they each become meaningless without the other. The sign of the cross contains and alludes to the Resurrection; the ascending movement of the hand shows the conquest of Jesus over death, and the gift of eternal life. Our connection with the instrument of the death of Jesus, the same instrument that conquered death, reminds us of our spiritual immortality, something that modern secular culture often resists facing. Perhaps never before have humans tried to fight against physical death as we do now. And when we cannot fight death, we try to hide it: An open casket funeral is a thing of the past.

The Resurrection of Jesus transformed the problem of death into a curable disease. The Crucifixion and Resurrection cured death—the effect of sin. The cross was seen as an instrument of salvation. This can be seen in the typological connection between Jesus on the cross and the bronze serpent that was held up on a pole that, when looked at, cured the Israelites.[44] By accepting and internalizing the cross of Christ through gesturing the sign of the cross, we acknowledge the immortality of our soul and our spiritual resurrection in Jesus Christ. Now it is something turned inside out: The cross, an instrument of and symbol of physical death, has become the symbol of eternal life.

We know there are two different kinds of death. The first, physical death, is defined as the separation of the body and the soul. This is a certainty we all fear; we fear the unknown. Most of us lack the spiritual insight and strength to see past this physical death, although some people such as Elder Porphyrios, a monk from Mt. Athos, have the long-sighted view. Before he died in the 1990s, he started building a chapel, at a very advanced age. Someone asked him why he was spending his labors in this way, since he was old and would surely die soon. The Elder answered him, "But I am not going to die, my child, Christ told me so." He was not naïve, and was very aware of his forthcoming physical death, but his faith gave him the wider view of eternal life in Paradise. He spoke to the church's view of the separation between body and soul as something temporary. The Creed ends with the phrase "I look for the resurrection of the dead," referring to the resurrection of our bodies after the Second Coming of Christ. For this reason, in the language of the church the expression "dormition" or "sleep" is used instead of "death."

The second kind of death is more terrifying. Spiritual death is separation from God, and this is the heaviest consequence of the fall of Adam and Eve. Jesus, by his death and resurrection, reversed this condition of spiritual death, however, and closed the gap between humanity and God.

The early church celebrated the resurrection of Christ more than any other feast. And now, every Sunday is considered a weekly celebration of the resurrection of Christ. The historical resurrection of Jesus was clearly important for the church, as we read in St. Paul's first letter to the Corinthians: "And if Christ has not been raised, our preaching is useless and so is your faith. More than that, we are then found to be false witnesses about God, for we have testified about God that he raised Christ from the dead. But he did not raise him if in fact the dead are not raised. For if the dead are not raised, then Christ has not been raised either. And if Christ has not been raised, your faith is futile; you are still in your sins." (1 Corinthians 15:14-17)

Yet, as the hymnography and the liturgical tradition of the church show, what the church celebrates is not so much the historical resurrection of Jesus as our own spiritual resurrection brought about by the historical resurrection.

In Byzantine tradition, an apocryphal text written in the fourth century, the Gospel of Nicodemus, expresses the spirituality of the Resurrection: the victory of Jesus over death—not just Jesus' own death—and the salvation of humanity. This text forms the basis for the Byzantine icon of the resurrection of Christ, describing Jesus' descent to Hades, where he liberates all the prophets of old who were expecting him, and all of humanity, and where he binds Death personified. In this icon of the Resurrection we see Jesus raising Adam and Eve and taking them by the hand. Jesus, the saints around him, and Adam and Eve seem victorious, whereas Death is represented as an old, beaten man in chains. Nothing about the historical resurrection of Christ appears in the icon, yet it represents the spiritual work of the resurrection: Christ raising humanity and conquering death.

The icon shows the raising of Adam and Eve, and by extension, the raising of all humanity. In later icons of the Resurrection, following the apocryphal text, there appears an added depiction of the righteous walking to heaven, where they are greeted by Enoch and Elijah, prophets who were taken up to heaven in their physical bodies without dying. The resurrection of the dead in this icon clearly suggests the spiritual resurrection. The iconography and hymnology of the church celebrate not only the resurrection of Christ, but foremost, its meaning: the spiritual resurrection of humanity.

Here is where our spiritual resurrection becomes a matter of the here and now, and an issue of prayer. The continuous resurrection of the church and our own spiritual renewal in Christ are accomplished within every liturgy when we partake of the body and blood of Jesus. The liturgy corresponds to the ascetic ascent of the Christian towards God, during which we keep falling, and God keeps raising us.

Christian literature is filled with images of struggling ascetics and monastics who go to unusual lengths to attain salvation and explore the limits of spiritual warfare. The life of laypeople is normally less extreme. For most of us, it is in the family, community, and workplace where we are called to fight our spiritual fight, be our brother's keeper, and assist our neighbor. We live in a fallen condition, and when we try to stay in the path of God the difficulties are enormous. Yet, God does not force salvation on us, but invites collaboration between humans and the divine, which is necessary for salvation: a synergy of the human and the divine—that is, the human and the divine act together to create an effect greater than the sum of the effects each is able to create independently.

In the Gospels, as well as in the writings of the Fathers, we see that there are certain virtues that attract the grace of God. In one instance, mercy is given where there is humility. This is shown in the parable of the tax collector and the Pharisee, where Jesus showed us that humility contributes to our salvation more than keeping the rules and regulations of the Law. While the Pharisee tried to reach God by ascending the ladder of God-given commandments, his own account of his pious works before God was not enough to win him entrance to the Kingdom of God.

The tax collector in the parable, realizing that his own moral strength was failing him, threw his pride aside and put his hope in the mercy of God. Here, salvation becomes a matter of spiritual death and resurrection.

In our everyday efforts we pray for forgiveness of our sins: In other words, we pray for spiritual resurrection. Placing ourselves into the images of the icon of the descent of Christ to Hades, we seal ourselves with the sign of the cross and humbly ask Jesus to raise us up again from sinfulness and from spiritual death, and to set us on his right side.

The sign of the cross on our body symbolizes the Resurrection through the upward movement of the hand. Most accounts suggest that this reflects a movement from the tomb to heaven and the Second Coming of Christ. But we also mark ourselves with the sign of Christ in order to share in spiritual resurrection and liberation from sin. With the sign of the cross we may meditate on spiritual death (seeing ourselves as dead to sin), then giving ourselves to Christ in humility, to cleanse our soul so that we may enter the Kingdom of Heaven with Christ.

The Second Coming of Christ

The cross figures heavily in the church's teaching about the final events in the history of the world. The phrase "sign of Christ" refers to the appearance of the cross before the Second Coming of Christ. In the book of Revelation this sign of the cross contrasts with the "sign of the beast."

The name or the symbol of Christ on our foreheads, as we saw in the history of the development of the sign of the cross, directly references the war that will take place at the end of time, described in the book of Revelation. By tracing the sign of the cross on our body, we position ourselves at the side of the Lamb in this war that takes place at the end of the age, and at the same time we accept our own judgment by Christ. We may think that a cosmic war sounds terrifying, but its favorable conclusion is known to us: the heavenly Jerusalem, the paradise that will be revealed at the end of time, bathed in eternal light, prepared for the righteous. And the sign of the cross that we gesture now, is an anticipation of this end; it is submission to the judgment and the will of God and participation in paradise restored.

The dimension of the sign of the cross that refers to the end of time seems simple enough: On the one hand, in its ancient form, traced over the forehead, the sign anticipates the mark of the righteous at the end of the age. The gesture of the sign, however, formed large over the body, suggests the differentiation between the right and the left side, in supplication to Christ the great Judge at the end of time, to place us on his right (the right side is always equated with the righteous), and not on his left, with the wicked.

The liturgy takes us to the end of time, as well, and the right hand of Christ. In what is one of the most spiritually charged moments of the Divine Liturgy, during the consecration of the bread and the wine, the priest addresses Christ and remembers all that he has accomplished for our salvation. The words of the liturgy read, "Having in remembrance, therefore, this saving commandment and all those things which have come to pass for us: the Cross, the Grave, the Resurrection on the third day, the Ascension into heaven, the Sitting at the right hand, and the second and glorious Coming, your own of your own we offer to you, in behalf of all, and for all."

This clue in the spiritual tradition of the church reveals its cosmic spiritual dimension, where, according to a certain reading of the liturgy, we are transposed immediately to the end of time, after the Second Coming, in the presence of God. The proclamation with which the liturgy starts, "Blessed is the Kingdom of the Father, and of the Son, and of the Holy Spirit, now and ever, and into the ages of ages," reminds us that the Kingdom of God is present, and from there on everything takes place in transfigured time, as if seen from the other end of our ascetic ascent. The original Greek word, βασιλεία, translated as "kingdom," is not geographically specific, unlike the word βασίλειον, which corresponds more precisely to "kingdom" as a place. Biblical and liturgical references to the Kingdom of God or the Kingdom of Heaven do not suggest a place so much as a placing of ourselves under the dominion of God, outside of time and space. And in the mystery and sacrament that gives us his body and blood in the Eucharist, God, in some way, transports us to the end of human history.

Central to the story of the end of time is the symbol of the cross. The "sign of the Son of Man" referred to in the Gospel of Matthew[45] was taken by the church to mean the symbol of the cross. And the cross figures in all literature about the end of time. In the influential though apocryphal gospel of Nicodemus that narrates the descent of Christ to Hades, there is a description of Christ applying the sign of the cross on the foreheads of Adam, the prophets and patriarchs of old, the forefathers, the martyrs and all the righteous in Hades, so that they may enter heaven. In this same text, the repentant thief, who was crucified next to Jesus and in humility asked to be with Jesus in paradise, was given entrance to heaven when the flaming sword of the angel— referring to the story told in the book of Genesis—was taken away. The angel who guarded the gates of Eden with the flaming sword forbade Adam and Eve's return to Eden. Yet, paradise was opened for the thief when the angel saw the sign of the cross.

Such images did not stay in the apocryphal texts, but infused the hymnology and the iconography of the church. A hymn from the Feast of the Exultation of the Cross declares that "the wood of the cross quenched the flaming sword at the gates of Paradise."

This sacramental transposition to the time after the Second Coming of Christ and the Last Judgment would normally fill us with awe and terror. Yet, the church has a joyful vision of this end of time. The sign of the cross placed us on the side of God, reflecting where the righteous desire to be. When we cross ourselves, we face and we invite the Judgment of Christ. By performing the sign of the cross during the liturgy, we recall and we relive the end of time, and we also recall our contrition before the throne of Christ. This moment is the culmination of all prayers, the moment anticipated by human history after the Fall, for which Jesus descended to earth in order to prepare us. Performing the sign of the cross we envision the apocalyptic "sign of the Son of Man," and bowing to it, we pray for the salvation of humanity.

*

One may question whether all this range of Christological symbolisms and connections really goes through the mind of the average Christian performing the sign of the cross upon entering a church or during the liturgy or in private prayer. It would be naïve to suggest that, but this is how symbols, icons, and signs operate: They keep within them a multitude of meanings that they were given intentionally and also unconsciously. Upon reflecting on these signs, the faithful find that these meanings are made available. The sign, as an act, however small it may be, expresses the impetus of cross-ing the threshold between *thinking* in theological terms and *practicing* the Christian life.

Certainly, living a faithful life is not just a matter of per-forming rituals and signs without internalizing and expanding them. Living in Christ is living in prayer, whether in the church, at home, or in the workplace. But most of us separate—rather than integrate—spiritual thought and spiritual practice, theology and prayer. Good deeds or active spirituality are meaningful when they flow naturally from the offering of the self to Christ, the church, and all the people.

For the church Fathers and the early Christians, the distinction between theology and prayer did not exist the way it does now. One of the famous maxims of Evagrius of Pontos states, "If you are a theologian, you pray correctly; and if you pray correctly you are a theologian." While Evagrius had the needs of the monastic community in mind, the layperson would see the end of separation between theology and prayer when living a life as an act of prayer. The sign of the cross is a symbol of this spiritual way, a seal of a life that is offered as a prayer to Jesus, not a life of separation, but of spiritual integration.

CHAPTER FIVE

The Cosmic Cross

"Cosmic Spirituality"

isit a mainstream bookstore, especially in North America, and peruse its section on religion and spirituality, and you'll get the distinct impression that religion and spirituality are almost mutually exclusive. It makes things more perplexing to see the religion section next to the self-help section. *Chicken Soup for the Soul* is a title that might be placed next to Augustine's *Confessions*, Gregory of Nyssa's *The Life of Moses*, and even the Bible.

Here on the shelves may be books from the New Age movement (often vilified to the level of a satanic plot by many people). The problem with such movements and books is that although they may start with good intentions, they often bring forth views and ideas that are presented as new to Western spirituality, when in fact they have either been discussed extensively and put aside by the church Fathers (such as belief in reincarnation), or they are part of the Christian tradition (such as meditative prayer). Nevertheless, the contribution of the New Age movement should not be limited to commonplace maxims such as "we are all one with the Cosmos" or "all is love," as many well-meaning writers and readers often come in contact for the first time with issues of real importance in the books of the movement. For people whose spiritual interest is more than skin deep, there are many books that inform and educate, and readers may seek out reputable books or take their questions to responsible individuals in the church for discussion. In this way they have the opportunity to see which ideas stand up to scrutiny and which do not. To that degree, New Age spirituality may have acted as an entry point for such seekers who would not normally have the chance to cultivate their spiritual interests.

Here, it is important to note that North American society has lived a strange paradox in the past decades. Many generations of immigrants lost their ethnic identity and religious heritage when they came to the New World, and lost with it their collective memory of development. And despite criticisms of popular spirituality, the phenomenon of a growing interest in New Age spirituality reveals two things: first, that traditional religions have distanced themselves from contemporary life or have not educated their faithful in their own traditions; and second, that people and generations who have grown up outside the church, have made an impressive statement in culture and as consumers, in this way indirectly making known their spiritual needs, seeking answers, and looking for genuine faith.

In this attempt to reclaim some part of modern spirituality, I would like to discuss the symbol and the sign of the cross in relation to the idea of cosmic spirituality. Instead of taking a stance against popular non-specific spirituality, it would be more fruitful to present views of a theology and a tradition that have stood the test of time.

"Cosmic spirituality" sounds like a New Age expression, but both words have signified something important in Christian tradition. The word "spirituality" is not simple to define. Contrary to paganism, which saw an irreconcilable distance between the body and the soul, from the beginning Christianity embraced the concepts of both the body and the soul as constituent parts of the self. Christianity did not view the body as the tomb of the soul, as depicted in Platonism. Nor was the body viewed as an insignificant vessel that could be discarded until the soul is reborn inside another body, as is the case in reincarnation beliefs. Rather, the resurrection we profess at the end of the Nicene Creed is the resurrection of our *bodies,* and until that happens we will be incomplete.

Some of the earliest heresies Christianity confronted had to do with the acceptance of the material world as a creation of God. Various Gnostic groups argued that the material world was inherently evil, and it had to have been created, therefore, by someone other than God.

Christianity regarded the body as an integral part of the self, created by the hands of God. Yet it is also true that the tradition of the church repeatedly exulted in everything spiritual, something we witness in the writings of the desert Fathers and in the church's hymnology. Still, this does not reflect the kind of opposition and contempt for the body and the material world that we find in a system of belief such as Platonism.

But how, then, does Christianity define the term "spiritual"? Christian tradition does not refer to a differentiation between matter and spirit; rather, the spiritual refers to the operation of the Holy Spirit. The spiritual in Christianity is not a negation of the material, but something beyond it. In a metaphoric way, the material world may also be part of the spiritual realm. These two are not mutually exclusive. God, as Jesus told the Samaritan woman in the Gospel of John, is spirit.[46] And just as we would not exclude God from his own creation, we could not claim that God is limited only to a bodiless or immaterial world.

In the Christian tradition "spiritual" has to do with being made holy, something that is achieved by the work of the Holy Spirit of God within the faithful. In this way, it is then possible to have spiritual bodies—for anyone touched by the work of the Holy Spirit is spiritual. Conversely, a soul that has not been touched by the Spirit of God may be viewed as non-spiritual.

The spiritual refers to a condition of inviting the spirit of God into our lives, living in the spirit, and sanctifying the world with it. Every Christian, to some extent, has been given what the first letter of Peter calls the "royal priesthood" of Christ,[47] and every Christian participates in the sanctification of the world in their everyday lives.

From the time it was first practiced by the early Christians, the sign of the cross has been used as a sign of sanctification. The sign of the cross was made by early Christians to sanctify food, the bed, each other, and themselves. Its significance is similar to the sign of priestly blessing; the sign of the cross is a sign of blessing used by laypeople. It is personal and also communal, with nothing secretive or "mystical" about it (in the sense of any kind of privileged knowledge). In this way it differs from notions of spirituality that imply a private, mystical connection with the divine.

The cross's spirituality is a spirituality of openness, of transforming the world and our actions, such as eating or sleeping. No moments are more spiritual than others if everything is done in the name of God. In addition, since the most usual way to perform the sign of the cross is over our body, we recognize that our body and our entire self may become temples of the Spirit of God. As a result, a life that is completely consecrated to God is considered more spiritual than life before the fall of Adam and Eve.

There are other rituals or symbols of the church that reflect the operation of the Holy Spirit of God in our life, such as baptism, marriage, and our sacramental Eucharistic union with the body of Jesus, but only the sign of the cross represents a continuously sacramental life, which reverses the consequences of the Fall. For this reason, the sign of the cross is the most "spiritual" of the symbols of the church.

"Cosmos" and "cosmic" are two terms that have been misused and misunderstood in modern parlance. For ancient Greeks the terms meant "order" and "beauty." In the Platonic tradition, the impressively wise order of the universe warranted this beautiful characterization. Indeed, we should have more reasons today to appreciate this word *cosmos*, based on what we know of the spectacular order of the created universe. The expressions "cosmos" and "cosmic" in modern popular spirituality have been used to refer to a type of pantheistic connection of the self and the universe. In many ways traditional Christianity reveals a very strong spiritual or metaphysical connection between humanity and the universe. On an initial level, we read about the fall of our forebears and see how this had cosmic repercussions: When humanity fell from the grace of paradise, the rest of creation was dragged behind, into the fallen condition. This is why nature now is not as it was in paradise, where, as the prophet Isaiah depicts the future end of time, once again "the wolf will dwell with the lamb, and the leopard will lie down with the kid."[48] Nature fell from grace, and it stays in that condition until that prophesied day.

The repercussions of the fall of our forebears were so grim not because humans introduced sin to the world (in some way that had already been done by Satan) but because of the special position God gave humanity. According to the tradition of the church, the human being stands in the middle of all creation, participating in the spiritual as well as in the material world. The place of humanity is therefore above that of angels, who are normally limited to the invisible world. The cosmic dimensions of humanity exceed anything we might imagine. In the tradition of the church the human being, therefore, is a small version of the entire universe—a *microcosm*, as the church Fathers called it. In perfected creation, humans would stand in the center, transmitting the will and the love of God to every corner of the world.

After the fall of humanity and of the natural world, though, humanity could not live up to its cosmic role. And the universe underwent one more big change after the Fall when nature itself participated in the mourning for the death of Jesus on the cross. The Gospel relates how when Jesus was crucified the sun eclipsed and the earth shook, and when Jesus expired people were resurrected from graves. This show of reaction by creation at this momentous event baffled even the angels. Icons of the Crucifixion symbolize this when they include representations of the sun and the moon on either side of the cross.

The cosmic order responded to the crucifixion of Christ. This response points to the cosmic dimensions of the return of humanity to God. This return to God was made possible by Jesus' crucifixion, which provided the template humanity needed in order to find its way through the fallen world. The Crucifixion also made possible the spiritual perfection, also called sanctification, of humanity, as well as the sanctification of nature, and the return to the condition of peace among all creatures, as existed before the Fall.

For this reason, many saints have, according to this sancti-fication, restored a contact and communication with animals. Perhaps the most famous example of this is St. Francis of Assisi, who preached to the animals. Ascetic Orthodox literature is also filled with examples of saints who lived with lions, such as St. Gerasimos of the desert, whose companion lion was named Jordan, or St. Mamas of Cyprus who was often seen coming down the mountains riding a lion. Such examples fore-shadow the cosmic significance of the salvation of humanity.

Such returns to a peaceful connection to animals were not accomplished because saints themselves were spiritual, though. The saints had no more power than that given them by God. Jesus Christ himself identified God the Father as the only source of goodness, divinity, and sanctity, as the Gospels attest.[49] The sanctification of humanity therefore is the work of the Holy Trinity, performed in collaboration with humanity.

Men and women who accept the beneficial power of God by attaching themselves to the Crucified Jesus are those who display this aspect of Christian faith.

Another important characteristic of the "cosmic" in Christianity is the personal connection of every Christian to God and to each other. Rather than the cosmos being an impersonal accumulation of diverse life forms, space and matter, it is the creation of God through Christ, given life by the Holy Spirit. The book of Genesis depicts this, showing how God the Father created the sun, the stars, the earth, plants, and animals through his spoken or breathed Word. The Creed refers to this creative act, and to Jesus who is called the Word, and "through whom all things were made." The universe, as far as Christianity is concerned, is nothing less than the boundless expression of the creative power of God, working through Christ. The Christian universe is profoundly Christocentric. And because of this, the universe is deeply personal.

From what we witness here, it is evident that "cosmic" and "spirituality" are not ethereal concepts, but integral parts of the Christian tradition. We also see how difficult it would be to consider the cosmic significance of humanity without reference to the sanctifying spirituality of the Holy Spirit. This relates directly to the sign of the cross, because as an inward symbol of acceptance, the sign accepts and invites the operation of the Holy Spirit—and consequently our sanctification and "spirituality." It accepts and invites the way of the cross—and so helps us attach ourselves to the crucified and resurrected Jesus, the one who became a bridge, between God and humanity. And the sign of the cross, by virtue of its symbolism, is the *axis mundi,* the axis or center of the world, reflecting further the convergence of the entire cosmos onto the microcosm of the human being.

The Cross as Axis Mundi

The cross is such an archetypal symbol that, even if we came from a completely alien culture, we would probably be able to deduce something of its significance. The cross is the simplest possible combination of two planes, and attracts attention precisely where these two planes have their cross-section. As an elementary shape, the cross makes a visual statement that could be put into words as "there is a vertical plane, a horizontal plane, and they meet." Before it was adopted by Christianity, the symbol of the cross, as well as similar designs, had been used by several cultures and religions to express spiritual beliefs. This does not make it any less of a Christian symbol. Although the cross existed before Jesus, the symbol was naturally adopted by his followers because of its historical connection with his death, but also because of the sign's ability to visually express some of Christianity's deepest beliefs.

Many religions viewed the polarity between earth and heaven as a way to express the polarity between the sacred and the profane, that is, temporal life and the afterlife, or the realm of mortals and the realm of the gods. For these religions the upward movement towards heaven was often accompanied or symbolized by a spiritual journey to the other world that often involved a death and a resurrection. In early animistic cultures this role was assumed by the shaman, who represented a person who died and passed to the other realm, where his dead body was reconstructed and then returned back to earth. The rituals of animistic cultures often symbolize these stages. The differentiation between the two realms was symbolized by a sacred pole or tree that somehow connected the two realms. The tree was seen as a sacred center that gave meaning to the world. As an *axis mundi* it provided the sacred principle necessary for social organization. And although in many cultures (such as in Norse, Celtic, Persian, and Slavic mythology) this *axis mundi* was symbolized by an actual tree (a symbolism handed down to our culture in the form of the Christmas tree) or mountain, it could have also been another kind of sacred site that confirmed these poles or provided the sought-after communication between heaven and earth. The famous oracle of Delphi in ancient Greece is an example of this; it was believed to be the genuine voice of the god Apollo and was also known as the "navel of the earth"— the same imagery many Jewish writers used to refer to and describe Jerusalem.

The cross, in some ancient and simple renderings, is a simple vertical pole. The language of the Crucifixion narratives suggests that the cross is the platform on which Jesus "ascended" or from which he "descended." The significance of the vertical dimension of the cross, and the fact that the Gospels often refer to it as ξύλον, "wood" or "tree," suggest a clear affinity with the archetypal pre-Christian symbolism of the axis of the world.

The ascent of Jesus on the cross paved the way for his resurrection and provided humanity the way of salvation: Spiritual ascent from the world of sin to the Heavenly Kingdom. Jesus established, through his death and resurrection, a connection between heaven and earth. This is symbolically similar to the shamanistic connections between the spiritual and the material realm. This should not surprise us: Jesus referred to himself as the connection between heaven and earth. At the beginning of his ministry, he promised his apostles, as recorded in the Gospel of John, that they will "see the heaven opened, and the angels of God ascending and descending upon the Son of Man."[50] The most significant moments in the work of Jesus took place on this vertical dimension, which we see reflected in the sign of the cross: his downward incarnation, his death and descent to Hades, his resurrection, and finally his ascension.

The other axis, which corresponds to the horizontal beam of the cross, is more difficult to interpret. According to the church Fathers, the image of Jesus with his arms stretched out on the cross is the image of Christ accepting and embracing humanity in his arms. This pictorial invitation points us to salvation through Christ. The Fathers have also compared the image of Jesus on the cross with the image of prayer—with the arms upward turning and outstretched—indicating the way to salvation. While such interpretations demonstrate the depth of this image of the crucified Jesus, let's look at the cross from a more basic level, as an elementary shape, without the body of Jesus on it.

In keeping with the symbolism of the cosmic significance of the vertical pole, the horizontal beam of the cross becomes an additional axis that extends to the ends of the world, East and West, North and South. Although the cross is normally a two-dimensional symbol, sometimes a second horizontal pole is added to it, perpendicular to the existing one. We see this type of cross decorating a church dome or steeple. The vertical pole alone is not a symbol strong enough to represent the continuous descent, or rather indwelling, of God in humanity, and the ascent of man. The addition of the horizontal beam places the supernatural connection of heaven and earth in the context of the liturgical community, gathered around the axis of ascent. In other words, while the vertical axis alone states that "there is a connection between heaven and earth," adding the horizontal axis modifies this statement to mean "there is a connection between heaven and earth, and it is offered to the entire world."

Placing the crossbeam to the vertical pole creates a sense of convergence. The two beams visually designate a powerful center point. The relation between the center and the sides of the cross is a relation of emanating and returning. This concept becomes evident when we draw a star in simple way. We draw a simple cross or an X, or even a combination of the two as in the asterisk (a word that literally means "little star"), using the sides of the cross to represent the rays of the star. This visual sense of emanating and returning, or converging, was more evident in early Christian crosses. The most common cross in early Christianity was the equilateral cross or "Greek cross," where this sense of convergence is relayed much stronger than in other types of cross.

Perhaps we are not accustomed to think about the cross primarily as an image of convergence. And while there is little to support this understanding, yet the symbol of the cross indicates a strong focal point that corresponds to the body of Jesus on the crucifix. In his act of salvation from the cross, Jesus invited all humanity. His crucifixion issued the invitation to salvation in the Gospel of John: "When I am lifted up from the earth [on the cross], I will draw all people to myself."[51]

The physical gesture of the sign of the cross on our body, understood in this context, resonates with the early Christian writers' understanding of the human being as a microcosm. The sign of the cross does not only symbolize the divine drama, but also the cosmic dimensions of this drama—heaven and the underworld. The higher and the lower parts of the world are "placed" on the higher and the lower parts of the body. This may be seen more clearly in the gesture of the "big cross," a combination of the sign of the cross and a prostration, where the faithful start the sign on their forehead, but instead of continuing with the belly, they bow and touch the floor instead.

The sign of the cross affirms the exceptional key position of the human being in the hierarchy of the cosmos. Its symbolism of the body as the center of the universe is evident, and this universe is not an impersonal one. The microcosm of the human being, which reflects the cosmos of creation, is clearly centered on Christ. And the center of this microcosm is defined by the cross, or the "sign of the Son of Man," as a sign that belongs both to us and to Christ.

The sign of the cross on our body demonstrates our belief in a Christocentric universe, connecting our rigorously self-disciplined ascent towards God with the cosmic salvation of the fallen creation. The heart, the focal center of the sign of the cross, for many ascetic Fathers of the church, represents the center of the self, the locus where the spiritual struggle takes place. By identifying our body with the universe, and by symbolically inviting Jesus Christ into the center of the microcosm that we are, we not only acknowledge the cosmic dimensions of our salvation, but we place our trust and hope for this salvation in the Cosmic Christ, through whom the entire universe was created.

The Cosmic Cross at the End of the World

The symbolic connection between heaven and earth, as expressed by the cross, was made concrete by the historic crucifixion of Jesus. The differentiation between heaven and earth is perhaps of the same type of differentiation between this age and the age after the Second Coming of Christ. The cross of Christ, symbolically bridging heaven and earth, can be seen as a connection between present time and the time of the end of the world. This was one reason why the cross was considered a symbol of the end of time by the early church. The significance of the image of the cross as a symbol of the end of the world was something early Christians were familiar with. Several people in the fourth century reported the apparition of a luminous cross over Jerusalem, and interpreted this vision as a sign that the Second Coming of Christ was imminent.

The cosmic dimension of the cross, as well as its use as the truest sign of Christ, meet together in a reference to "the sign of the Son of Man"[52] coming at the end of the world. This reference in a passage from Matthew's Gospel has great importance for the early church's anticipating the Second Coming of Christ. Therefore, this passage of Matthew was given higher status as an account of the end of the world than passages from the book of Revelation, which was neither read liturgically in church nor as widely known and studied.

The impact of the cross as the apocalyptic "sign of Man" can be seen in the cross's depiction in early Christian art. Most early church apse representations have a triumphal character showing the end of the world, drawing attention to this message, because the apse formed the focal point of services. In the earlier understanding of liturgical processions, the "sign of man" symbolized heaven, salvation, and the future end of the world. A special representation of the cross, one that has an explicitly apocalyptic character, can be found featured in many early churches. One well-known example is the early fifth-century apse mosaic in the church of St. Pudenziana in Rome. In this mosaic Christ is depicted in glory. Seated with him are his apostles, ready to judge the masses, according to Jesus' promise to them that when he sits on the throne of his glory, they will also sit on twelve thrones, judging the twelve tribes of Israel.[53] Behind the apostles we see four winged beasts surrounding a huge bejeweled cross, placed against a background of clouds. The cross here dominates the scene, as prominent as Christ, and portrayed on a visual plane above him.

Images of the cross surrounded by many stars, such as the ones in the churches of Galla Placidia and San Vitale in

Ravenna, also point to the cross's cosmic, end-time character. The cross in this setting is represented as a huge luminous sign against the starry sky, as if replacing the sun and the moon. The stars, in these images, visually refer to the fall of the stars from the sky and the destruction of the known world, events which according to the book of Revelation precede the Second Coming of Christ. In this scale the cross is as big as the universe. And the cross has appeared when everything else has been destroyed—as though the outer part of the world were stripped away, revealing what is underneath: the seal of Creation, the sign of Jesus the Word: a big, luminous cross.

The Healing Cross

The cosmic significance of the cross may be seen from yet another perspective. Within its context of the end of the world, the cross is not an instrument of suffering or punishment, but a sign of healing, grace, and forgiveness. This is most clearly seen in the apocryphal Gospel of Nicodemus, mentioned previously. In this account, which offers a spiritual reading of Jesus' resurrection, the cross is presented as the means by which death and Satan are conquered. In that same narrative, the first person to enter Paradise after the resurrection of Christ is the repentant thief. The narrative hints at the idea that the repentant thief shared Jesus' suffering. It was not, though, through his own suffering that the thief reached paradise. Only the cross of Christ could open the gates of paradise. In the narrative, the repentant thief carries "the sign of the cross," in reference to Christ's cross, rather than his own.

This same idea, presented poetically in a Byzantine hymn from the third Sunday of Great Lent, points to the "adoration of the life-giving cross." The hymn affirms that "the fiery sword no longer guards the gate of Eden, for in a strange and glorious way the wood of the cross has quenched its flames." As noted before, this fiery sword refers to the angel who, according to the book of Genesis, was placed by God to guard the gates of paradise after the expulsion of Adam and Eve. According to medieval tradition and poetry, the cross was the antidote for the banishment of humanity from paradise.

Late medieval tradition connects the wood of the cross with the wood of the tree of Good and Evil, the tree associated with original sin. According to this medieval legend, the wood of the fateful tree of Good and Evil was preserved by Adam, passed on to the patriarchs, and at some point was lost. Later it was found and was used to fashion the cross of Christ. This legend grew around the theological connection between Adam and Christ. The church sometimes called Christ the New Adam, the one who reversed the consequences of the fall of the first Adam. The connection of the tree to the cross suggests the same connection.

This legend, as well as the apocryphal writing of Nicodemus, drawing attention to the association between the wood of the cross and the flaming sword of the angel guarding the gates of paradise, demonstrate the theology of Jesus' crucifixion. The Crucifixion enacted the expiation of original sin, reversing the Fall. In typically medieval logic, the instrument of healing and salvation was seen to be naturally related to the instrument of the fall of humanity.

While some may dismiss this medieval reasoning as too naïve for modern scientific theology, let us look closer at what this association intends to tell us. In these stories, salvation is achieved by a return to the problem of original sin. The sacrifice of Jesus on the wood of the cross was viewed in medieval times as the "correction" of the transgression, made by taking the fruit of the tree of Good and Evil. As a result, the true dimensions of the cross stretch from the beginning to the end of time, and connect us with the sin of Adam and Eve.

In this light, the spiritual significance of the cross is nothing less than the undoing of original sin. Although all of us may experience a personal reconciliation with God, we do not have the ability to reach all the way to heaven. We do have the opportunity, however, to ascend to the cross, that is, to place ourselves in the hands of Jesus, who bridged the distance between heaven and earth for us. The cross is something like a spiritual portal to the Kingdom of God, the way through the narrow gate that Jesus spoke of. The sign of the cross offers us the opportunity to make the same proclamation as the repentant thief did, when he "carried the sign of the cross on his shoulders."

By the sign of the cross we accept Jesus' operation of spiritual healing, and we present ourselves symbolically to the angel who guards the gates of paradise, once we have been sealed by the seal of Christ. The connection between the wood of the cross and the wood of the tree of good and evil suggests that the salvation we seek by the cross cancels, in some ways, the consequences of the original sin, and therefore restores us to the condition of Adam and Eve in the Garden of Eden.

One of the most revealing theological commentaries on the economy of salvation is found in the Gospel of John, explaining further the difficult concept of original sin and its undoing: "No one has ascended to heaven but he who came down from heaven, that is, the Son of Man who is in heaven. And as Moses lifted up the serpent in the wilderness, even so must the Son of Man be lifted up, that whoever believes in him should not perish but have eternal life. For God so loved the world that he gave his only begotten Son, that whoever believes in him should not perish but have everlasting life. For God did not send his Son into the world to condemn the world, but that the world through him might be saved."[54]

In one of the few typological images offered in the Gospels—in which an event in the Hebrew Scriptures foreshadows another in the Christian Testament—the crucified Christ is compared to the bronze serpent that saved the Israelites when they met with the consequences of their sin. The book of Numbers tells us this story:

> Then they journeyed from Mount Hor by the way of the Red Sea, to go around the land of Edom; and the soul of the people became very discouraged on the way. And the people spoke against God and against Moses: "Why have you brought us up out of Egypt to die in the wilderness? For there is no food and no water, and our

soul loathes this worthless bread." So the Lord sent fiery serpents among the people, and they bit the people; and many of the people of Israel died. Therefore the people came to Moses, and said, "We have sinned, for we have spoken against the Lord and against you; pray to the Lord that He take away the serpents from us." So Moses prayed for the people. Then the Lord said to Moses, "Make a fiery serpent, and set it on a pole; and it shall be that everyone who is bitten, when he looks at it, shall live." So Moses made a bronze serpent, and put it on a pole; and so it was, if a serpent had bitten anyone, when he looked at the bronze serpent, he lived.[55]

John the Evangelist chose this passage from the book of Numbers to explain the mystery of humanity's salvation by Jesus. Here, the act of salvation was the Crucifixion. This salvation that humanity longed for was found when the consequences of the Fall were finally reversed. The connection of the Crucifixion with the bronze serpent tells us something of the nature and consequence of the sin that the cross and the bronze serpent healed. It also tells us of the way God acts to help humanity. In both instances, the sin consisted of humanity's disobedience, which resulted in a movement away from God. In both cases—the serpent and the tree of good and evil—the immediate result was death, physical and spiritual, the result of original sin.

Original sin is implied in the passage from Numbers, as well. In that narrative, the symbol of salvation and spiritual healing—the bronze serpent—was made in imitation of the exact thing that was causing death: deadly fiery serpents, punishment sent by God for the Israelites' sin.

The image of the serpent however, appears earlier in Scripture, in the book of Genesis, where the memory of Satan as the serpent in the Garden of Eden is still fresh. Clearly the serpent symbolizes the original transgression, and by extension, all sin. The plight of the Israelites later in their history is a reprise of the first time humanity was punished by being given over to the power of the serpent. The new element that this narrative in Numbers introduces is the cure, which comes, surprisingly enough, bearing the image of the sin, something that would have been seen as a scandal, that the cause of the disease could have had any part in the cure.

The cure of the Israelites by the bronze serpent, however, was not nearly as scandalous as the image of the Crucifixion. One of the reasons for which death by crucifixion was especially shameful for the Jews, is that the man who was hanged or crucified was considered cursed, as the book of Deuteronomy states: "If a man has committed a sin deserving of death, and he is put to death, and you hang him on a tree, his body shall not remain overnight on the tree, but you shall surely bury him that day, so that you do not defile the land which the Lord your God is giving you as an inheritance; for he who is hanged is accursed of God."[56] St. Paul referred to this text when he spoke of the scandal of the cross to the Corinthians and when he explained it further to the Galatians, writing, "Christ has redeemed us from the curse of the law, having become a curse for us, for it is written, 'Cursed is everyone who hangs on a tree.'"[57]

The scandal of the bronze serpent and the scandal of Christ's crucifixion were seen as such for good reason. The Israelites were cured of their affliction after they repented and asked God, through Moses, to be healed. The bronze serpent they had to look upon in order to be healed, represented the nature of their sin. This looking at the serpent and this healing of the body were not achieved without the necessary corresponding spiritual healing: The power of the bronze serpent to heal was based on the act of repentance and humility before God. True repentance could be achieved when the Israelites acknowledged their sin and understood its nature.

In the same way, the scandal and the curse of Jesus crucified connected deeply with the concept of original sin. The cross represents the remedy of humanity's sin. Jesus ascended to the cross in order to offer himself to those who, gazing upon him like the Israelites in the desert, acknowledge their sins, recognize their spiritual death and their separation from God, and ask to be reunited to him. For this reason, especially to those in the early church, the image of Christ on the cross was an image of triumph. Christ, in his death, triumphed over sin, and the contemplation of the triumphant crucified Christ is the way leading to our salvation. As the Resurrection Hymn of the Orthodox Church reminds us, "Christ trampled down death by death." The sign of the cross offers us this contemplation: a way to internalize the scandal of the cross and a way to seek reunion with God and the crucified Christ.

The consequences of original sin are presented as a disease in need of healing. "Healing" is exactly the proper expression in the passage from the book of Numbers, and apparently the Gospel of John connects the Crucifixion with the Numbers text precisely in order to make this clear. According to the Eastern Fathers, the expression "original sin" does not refer to an inherited sin that is passed biologically to every generation, but a disease that has plagued humanity since the fall of Adam and Eve. John's Gospel makes the same association: The Numbers passage, in which the afflicted person was healed by looking at the bronze serpent, foreshadows the healing of the sinful, fallen condition of humanity by the Crucifixion of Christ.

We may ask what the difference is between this view of original sin as not inherited, but as a disease, a plague on humanity, and the widespread notion of original sin as something we inherit, already carrying it when we are born. By way of practical difference, these may look similar: In both cases we are born into a world of sin, which is the direct result of the transgression of our forebears. What makes all the difference, however, is that if original sin is seen as a disease and not as a biologically or otherwise inherited personally held sin, there is no collective transmission of guilt. We may be tainted by original sin, but not the original guilt. Strange as this may seem, there is little room for guilt in Christianity. The Greek word for sin, αμαρτία, means literally "to miss the mark," suggesting that sin harms primarily the one who commits sin, who yields no real gain from it anyway. Guilt is the result of an unresolved condition, where the sin has not been expiated and the sinner has not reconciled with God.

On our own, we do not have the strength to abstain from sin, because we are born into the disease of sin. There is no reason to think that we can achieve sanctity based on our own power. As John the Evangelist reminds us before his writing about Christ and the bronze serpent: "No one has ascended to heaven but he who came down from heaven." He makes it clear that nobody achieves salvation on their own, but only through Christ. Guilt can be resolved when the sinner reconciles to God through repentance and the sacrament of confession. Jesus, as the second Adam, introduced the medicine, whereas the first Adam introduced the disease.

I still remember how relieved I felt when I understood the ramification of this theological view that separates original sin—or every sin for that matter—from the weight of humanity's guilt.

Those two biblical passages we examined say something important. Jesus, while remaining sinless himself, descended to the sinful condition of humanity in order to save us. He embraced and forgave the consequences of sin; he even took on the formal gown of curse and sin, without sinning himself. For our part, repentance, the contemplation of our sinful condition, and the true and profound invocation of the help of Jesus are necessary for forgiveness.

The sign of the cross is a reflection of this medicine given to us by Christ. It is a sign of contemplation on our sin, and as such it combines humility and the wish to triumph over sin and temptation. At the same time, it recognizes our own limitations and requests the assistance of God in our spiritual ascent and maturation. The sign of the cross reflects our personal commitment to healing the disease of sin and the consequences of the Fall. It is one of the first steps in our return towards God: Since we recognize our position and we place ourselves in his mercy and guidance, we, like the Israelites in the desert, may be healed of spiritual death.

*

We have examined many different aspects of the spirituality of the sign of the cross. We have looked at the sign of the cross as a profession of faith and as a symbol of the faith. The sign of the cross reveals the name of Christ and recapitulates his work of salvation. The cross is a symbolic connection between heaven and earth and a symbol of death to the world and our resurrection in Jesus Christ. The sign of the cross points to the Last Judgment and is an instrument of salvation and healing against the consequences of the Fall and original sin. The cross signifies personal and also communal worship, and it inspires wordless prayer.

All these aspects may not come to mind when we cross ourselves, but in the tacit symbolism of the humble sign we make all of these aspects part of our worship, and when we make the sign of the cross, we may bring them forth and be inspired by them.

What started as an exploration of the sign that was liberally gestured as blessing and consecration in early Christianity, ended with the sign's connection to cosmic spirituality and the mystery of salvation. This is often the case with elements of our liturgical life: We may start with a simple gesture or an iconographic nuance, and in seeking to understand the depth of its symbolism we may be led to profound mysteries of the faith.

The simple sign of the cross is one way of many to pray and at the same time to contemplate, as all prayer does, the mystery of the Father, the Son, and the Holy Spirit.

ACKNOWLEDGMENTS

Many people helped me during the writing of this book, and I would like to acknowledge their assistance and support here. Deborah Belonick was the first to suggest to me the idea of a book on the sign of the cross, and she put me in touch with Paraclete Press, who had already been thinking about such a project. Lil Copan, my editor, offered me a constructive perspective at every turn, from which the text benefited greatly. This book would not be the same without her. Terri Neimann lent me an additional pair of eyes and gave me a lot of support from the Pacific shore. Above all, I would like to thank Pavlos Rigas and Androulla Haalboom, who sustained me with their fraternal love in times of difficulty.

Behr, John. *The Mystery of Christ: Life in Death*. Crestwood, NY: SVS Press, 2006.

Bloom, Anthony. *Courage to Pray*. New York: Paulist Press, 1972.

Blowers, Paul, ed.. *Maximus the Confessor: On the Cosmic Mystery of Jesus Christ*. Crestwood, NY: SVS Press, 2004.

Bunge, Gabriel. *Earthen Vessels: The Practice of Personal Prayer According to the Patristic Tradition*. San Francisco: Ignatius Press, 2002.

Ghezzi, Bert. *The Sign of the Cross: Recovering the Power of the Ancient Prayer*. Chicago, IL: Loyola Press, 2004

Mathewes-Green, Frederica. *First Fruits of Prayer: A Forty-Day Journey through the Canon of St. Andrew*. Brewster, MA: Paraclete Press, 2005.

———. *The Open Door: Entering the Sanctuary of Icons and Prayer*. Brewster, MA: Paraclete Press, 2004.

Stewart-Sykes, Alistair, ed. *Tertullian, Cyprian and Origen: On the Lord's Prayer*. Crestwood, NY: SVS Press, 2004.

Ward, Benedicta, ed. *Lives of the Desert Fathers: The Historia Monachorum in Aegypto*. Lincoln, RI: Andrew Mowbray Publishers, 1981.

Ware, Kallistos. *The Power of the Name: The Jesus Prayer in Orthodox Spirituality*. Kalamazoo, MI: Cistercian Publications, 1986.

Williams, Rowan. *The Dwelling of the Light: Praying with Icons of Christ*. Norwich, U.K.: Canterbury Press, 2003.

———. *Ponder These Things: Praying With Icons of the Virgin*. Brewster, MA: Paraclete Press, 2006.

Chapter 1: Experiencing the Sign of the Cross

1. The earliest testimony for this may be found in the early third century, in Marcus Minutius Felix, *Apology for Christians*, 29.

Chapter 2: The Sign of the Cross: Its History

2. The discussion on doctrines and teachings can be found in Basil's *On the Holy Spirit*, 27, 188.

3. Tertullian's passage on the sign can be found in *De Corona*, 3.

4. This passage can be found in a work in which Cyril of Jerusalem discusses the importance of the cross, in *Catechetical Lecture 13*, 36.

5. Origen's comment on the *tau* can be found in *Select. in Ezek*. c. 9.

6. Examples of early depictions with an X on the forehead may be found in Alfoldi, A., and Alfoldi, E., *Die Kontorniat-Medaillons*, New York: Walter de Gruyter, 1990, vol. 2, 324.

7. The passage where Justin Martyr discusses the symbolism of the cross and the X can be found in his *Apology* 60, PG 6, 447.

8. The testimony about the luminous cross on the sky and the conversion of Constantine may be found in Eusebius of Caesarea, *Life of Constantine*, 1, 28–31.

9. Augustine's comment can be found in his *Tractatus CXVIII in John*, 5.

10. The valuable testimony on the instructions of Pachomius can be found in Palladius, *Lausiac History*, 32, 3.

11. Many examples where the cross is used as a weapon against demons can be found in monastic and ascetic literature. Cf. for instance, Athanasius of Alexandria, *Life of Anthony*, 13, 23, 35, 78, 80.

12. Monophysitism (belief in one nature) was a heresy that tormented the church in the fifth and sixth centuries. The disagreement was about the divine and the human nature of Christ, and how they relate to each other. The Fourth Ecumenical Council, held in Chalcedon in 451, tried to put a stop to the heresy, affirming belief in the two natures of Christ. The dispute did not end there, unfortunately, and further attempts to express the Monophysitic position ensued, known as Monoenergism (belief in one operation) and Monothelitism (belief in one will). The Oriental Orthodox Churches have remained formally separated from the Roman Catholic and the Eastern Orthodox Churches since 451, although it is now generally accepted that their theological positions are not Monophysitic.

13. John's original text reads as follows: [Ο σταυρός] ημίν σημείον δέδοται επί του μετώπου, ον τρόπον τω Ισραήλ η περιτομή. Δι΄ αυτού γαρ οι πιστοί των απίστων αποδιιστάμεθά τε και γνωριζόμεθα—Exposition of the Orthodox Faith, 4, 9, 27.

14. What Thurston took as the earliest testimony for a large cross comes from fourth-century Georgia, in the account of a miraculous healing performed by St. Nino, where after she prayed, "she took her (wooden) cross and with it touched the queen's head, her feet and her shoulders, making the sign of the cross and straightway she was cured" (Studia Biblica, V, 32). This does not necessarily suggest that the large cross had in any way replaced the cross on the forehead. St. Nino crossed the entire body of the ailing queen praying for a miracle on her body, which is probably more similar to the practice of performing the sign of the cross as a blessing over certain things.

15. John Chrysostom makes that comment in his Homily in Matthaeum LIV-LV, PG 58, 537.

16. The revealing testimony of Peter of Damascus on the sign of the cross may be found in his Book 1, "On the Differences between Thoughts and Provocations," *Philokalia*, vol. 3, Athens, 1960, 110.

17. The instructions of Leo IV to his clergy can be found in his *Homily*, PL 115, 677-678.

18. Innocent III offers his testimony and comments in his *De Sacro Altaris Mysterio*, II, 45, PL 217, 825.

19. The sign of the name of Christ, which is used as a sign of blessing by priests and bishops in the Orthodox Church, consists of the thumb and the fourth finger crossing, the index finger straight up, and the third and fifth finger slightly bent. The effect is that the index finger is seen as an I, the third as a C, the crossed thumb and fourth as an X, and the fifth as a C. The five fingers thus make up the letters ICXC, the first and last letters of the words Jesus Christ in Greek.

20. This challenging comment of Maximos the Greek can be found in *Sochinenija*, vol. I, 161, in Haney, J., *From Italy to Muscovy, the Life and Works of Maxim the Greek*, Munich: Wilhelm Fink, 973, 127.

21. An example of the sign of the cross being performed over the mouth can be found in Jerome's *Letter to Eustochium*, CVIII, 28, PL 22, 904. Another example where the sign of the cross is performed over the heart can be found in John Chrysostom's *Homily in Matthaeum* LXXXVII, PG 58, 771.

Chapter 3: The Need for Symbols and Signs

22. "I watched till thrones were put in place, and the Ancient of Days was seated; his garment was white as snow, and the hair of his head was like pure wool. His throne was a fiery flame, its wheels a burning fire" Daniel 7:9.

23. The discussion of symbolism and icons, and the reference to this category of icons can be found in John of Damascus, *Three Treatises on the Divine Images: St. John of Damascus*, Andrew Louth, trans. Crestwood, NY: St. Vladimir's Seminary Press, 2003, 99-100.

24. The testimony of Gregory Melissenos can be found in Sylvester Syropoulos, *Vera historia*, ed. p. 109, in Cyril Mango (ed.), *The Art of the Byzantine Empire*, University of Toronto Press, 1986, p. 254.

25. Christian priests still pray in this way in the liturgy, in the East and the West, having inherited this gesture of prayer from the Jews. A frequently used Lenten hymn repeats the verses of Psalm 141 and proclaims "Let my prayer be set forth before thee as incense; and the lifting up of my hands as the evening sacrifice."

26. "If any man will come after me, let him deny himself, and take up his cross, and follow me" Matthew 16:24.

27. "I have been crucified with Christ and I no longer live, but Christ lives in me" Galatians 2:20.

28. "If you want to be perfect, go, sell what you have and give to the poor, and you will have treasures in heaven; and come, follow me" Matthew 19:21.

29. This powerful image can be found in Pseudo-Macarius, *The Fifty Spiritual Homilies*, 2, homily 8.

Chapter 4: A Prayer to Christ

30. "Do not be anxious about anything, but in everything, by prayer and petition, with thanksgiving, present your requests to God. And the peace of God, which transcends all understanding, will guard your hearts and your minds in Christ Jesus" Philippians 4:6–7.

31. "Rejoice always, pray without ceasing, in everything give thanks; for this is the will of God in Christ Jesus for you" 1 Thessalonians 5:16–18.

32. "We do not know what we should pray for as we ought, but the Spirit himself makes intercession for us with groanings which cannot be uttered. Now he who searches the hearts knows what the mind of the Spirit is, because he makes intercession for the saints according to the will of God" Romans 8:26–27.

33. The connection between prayer and fasting may be seen in Matthew 17:21 and in Mark 9:29.

34. "Not my will, but yours, be done" Luke 22:42.

35. "Your Father knows the things you have need of before you ask him" Matthew 6:8.

36. "If I pray in a tongue, my spirit prays, but my understanding is unfruitful. What is the conclusion then? I will pray with the spirit, and I will also pray with the understanding. I will sing with the spirit, and I will also sing with the understanding" 1 Corinthians 14:14–15.

37. Readers who would like to know more about hesychasm can find a good introductions in John Meyendorff's *St. Gregory Palamas and Orthodox Spirituality*, Crestwood, NY: SVS Press, 1997, and *A Study of Gregory Palamas*, Crestwood, NY: SVS Press, 1998.

38. A short and very informative book on the Jesus prayer is Kallistos Ware, *The Power of the Name: the Jesus Prayer in Orthodox Spirituality*, Kalamazoo, MI: Cistercian Publications, 1986.

39. A good source for the life and teachings of St. Silouan is Archimandrite Sophrony, *Saint Silouan the Athonite*, Crestwood, NY: SVS Press, 1999.

40. The fifteenth-century reference of the Bridgettine nuns of Sion to the sign of the cross can be found in Blunt, John Henry (ed.), *Thomas Gascoigne: The Myroure of Oure Ladye*, Millwood, NY: Kraus Reprint Co., 1973, 80.

41. "I have been crucified with Christ; it is no longer I who live, but Christ lives in me; and the life which I now live in the flesh I live by faith in the Son of God, who loved me and gave himself for me" Galatians 2:20.

42. "If we have been united together in the likeness of his death, certainly we also shall be in the likeness of his resurrection, knowing this, that our old man was crucified with him, that the body of sin might be done away with, that we should no longer be slaves of sin. For he who has died has been freed from sin" Romans 6:5–7.

43. "When I am lifted up from the earth, I will draw all people to myself" John 12:32.

44. "And as Moses lifted up the serpent in the wilderness, even so must the Son of Man be lifted up, that whoever believes in him should not perish but have eternal life" John 3:14–15.

45. "Then the sign of the Son of Man will appear in heaven, and then all the tribes of the earth will mourn, and they will see the Son of Man coming on the clouds of heaven with power and great glory" Matthew 24:30.

46. "God is Spirit, and those who worship him must worship in spirit and truth" John 4:24.

47. "But you are a chosen generation, a royal priesthood, a holy nation, his own special people, that you may proclaim the praises of him who called you out of darkness into his marvelous light" 1 Peter 2:9.

Chapter 5: The Cosmic Cross

48. "The wolf also shall dwell with the lamb, the leopard shall lie down with the young goat, the calf and the young lion and the fatling together; and a little child shall lead them" Isaiah 11:6.

49. "Why do you call me good? No one is good but one, that is, God" Matthew 19:17, Mark 10:18, and Luke 18:19.

50. "Most assuredly, I say to you, hereafter you shall see heaven open, and the angels of God ascending and descending upon the Son of Man" John 1:51.

51. "When I am lifted up from the earth [on the cross], I will draw all people to myself" John 12:32.

52. "Then the sign of the Son of Man will appear in heaven, and then all the tribes of the earth will mourn, and they will see the Son of Man coming on the clouds of heaven with power and great glory" Matthew 24:30.

53. "Assuredly I say to you, that in the regeneration, when the Son of Man sits on the throne of his glory, you who have followed me will also sit on twelve thrones, judging the twelve tribes of Israel" Matthew 19:28, with a similar rendering in Luke 22:30.

54. "No one has ascended to heaven but he who came down from heaven, that is, the Son of Man who is in heaven. And as Moses lifted up the serpent in the wilderness, even so must the Son of Man be lifted up, that whoever believes in him should not perish but have eternal life. For God so loved the world that he gave his only begotten Son, that whoever believes in him should not perish but have everlasting life. For God did not send his Son into the world to condemn the world, but that the world through him might be saved" John 3:13–17.

55. "Then they journeyed from Mount Hor by the way of the Red Sea, to go around the land of Edom; and the soul of the people became very discouraged on the way. And the people spoke against God and against Moses: 'Why have you brought us up out of Egypt to die in the wilderness? For there is no food and no water, and our soul loathes this worthless bread.' So the Lord sent fiery serpents among the people, and they bit the people; and many of the people of Israel died. Therefore the people came to Moses, and said, 'We have sinned, for we have spoken against the Lord and against you; pray to the Lord that He take away the serpents from us.' So Moses prayed for the people. Then the Lord said to Moses, 'Make a fiery serpent, and set it on a pole; and it shall be that everyone who is bitten, when he looks at it, shall live.' So Moses made a bronze serpent, and put it on a pole; and so it was, if a serpent had bitten anyone, when he looked at the bronze serpent, he lived" Numbers 21:4–10.

56. "If a man has committed a sin deserving of death, and he is put to death, and you hang him on a tree, his body shall not remain overnight on the tree, but you shall surely bury him that day, so that you do not defile the land which the Lord your God is giving you as an inheritance; for he who is hanged is accursed of God" Deuteronomy 21:22-23.

57. "Christ has redeemed us from the curse of the law, having become a curse for us, for it is written, 'Cursed is everyone who hangs on a tree'" Galatians 3:13.

Aleph 19-20

Ancient of Days 49-148

Anthony the Great 21, 76-79

Antioch 24

Ascension of Christ 94-95, 109, 123

Athanasius of Alexandria 76-77

Augustine of Hippo 20-21, 113

Avvakum 35

Axis mundi 121-122

Basil the Great xvi, 11-12

Catholic xv, 22, 37, 56, 82

Christogram 18, 52

Constantine the Great 7, 17-18, 52, 54, 57, 80-81

Constantinople 41, 53, 57

Cosmic xvi, 108-109, 113-114, 117-120, 123, 125-126, 128, 137, 141

Crucifixion of Christ 5, 8, 23-24, 33, 43, 50, 75, 77, 81-82, 95, 99-103, 119, 122, 125-126, 129, 132-135

Cyril of Jerusalem 13-14, 23-24, 41

Damascus 23-26, 41, 53

Dionysius the Areopagite 66-67

Eucharist xi, xv, 8, 47, 53, 56, 64-65, 67, 101-102, 110, 117

Eusebius of Caesarea 17

Evagrius of Pontos 79, 90, 112

Exodus, Book of 49, 52

Filioque 31-32

Forehead ix, xi, 2, 12-17, 21-23, 25-26, 30, 40-41, 95, 99, 108, 110, 125

Gospel of Nicodemus (apocryphal) 105, 110, 128-129

Gospels x-xii, 3, 12, 19, 31, 74-75, 78, 84, 86-89, 95-97, 101, 107, 110, 116, 118-119, 122-123, 125, 127, 131, 135

Gregory Melissenos 54-57

Holy Trinity ix, 2-3, 5, 31-34, 37-39, 41, 49, 53, 72, 84-85, 98, 119-120

Iconoclasm 27-30, 51-52, 65

Incarnation of Christ 4, 46, 50, 86, 94-95, 97-99, 123

Innocent III (Pope) 34, 36, 41

Irenaeus of Lyons 7

Jesus prayer 91-93, 141

John Chrysostom xvi, 24, 94

John of Damascus 23, 25, 41, 53

Justin Martyr 7, 17

Kosmas Aitolos 39, 42, 84-85, 92, 94

Leo IV (Pope) 31, 33, 41

Lord's Prayer 4, 72, 88-89, 141

Makarian homilies 79-80, 90

Maximos (Trivolis) the Greek 35, 39

Minoan horns of consecration 50, 69-71

Monophysitism 22-23, 26

Moses 17, 38, 49, 113, 131-132, 134

Muslims 25-27, 39, 71

Myroure of Our Ladye 94-95

Numbers, Book of 131-135

Old Believers 30, 34-35

Origen 16, 20, 42, 141

Original sin 129-132, 134-137

Orthodox ix-x, xiii-xv, 1, 35-36, 39, 46, 56-57, 82, 90, 119, 134, 141

Pachomius 21, 81

Paul 6, 74, 86-87, 89, 100, 133

Peter of Damascus 24-26, 41

Plato 15, 17, 90, 115, 117

Prayer xii, 3-4, 7, 9, 16, 28, 39, 42, 46-47, 57-58, 61, 64, 70-74, 79, 84-93, 95, 97-100, 102, 106, 111-113, 123, 137-138, 141

Resurrection of Christ 4, 51, 85-86, 92, 95, 100, 103-107, 109, 123, 128, 134

Revelation, Book of 15-16, 20, 22,
    61, 64, 108, 127-128
Rome xv, 32, 41, 127
Second Coming of Christ 4, 36, 64,
    86, 104, 107-110, 126-128
Semiotics 29, 43, 45-47, 54
Serpent 103, 131-134, 136
Seventh Ecumenical Council 53
Sign of the Son of Man 110-111,
    125-127
Signified 45-49
Signifier 45-47, 49
Silouan the Athonite 94

Spirituality xiii, xvi, 12, 36, 47, 57,
    59, 61, 71, 74, 77-78, 84, 96, 105,
    111, 113-114, 116-118, 120, 137,
    141
Stoglav Council 35-36
Symbolism xvi-xvii, 5, 9, 18, 20, 24,
    31, 37-38, 40, 44, 46-47, 49, 53,
    56, 60, 62, 65-66, 68-69, 78, 80,
    94-95, 111, 121-125, 137
Tau 16, 19-20
Tertullian x-xi, 7, 13, 17, 42, 141
Thurston, Herbert 22-23
Truth (emet) 19-20

About Paraclete Press
Who We Are

Paraclete Press is an ecumenical publisher of books and recordings on Christian spirituality. Our publishing represents a full expression of Christian belief and practice—from Catholic to Evangelical, from Protestant to Orthodox.

Paraclete Press is the publishing arm of the Community of Jesus, an ecumenical monastic community in the Benedictine tradition. As such, we are uniquely positioned in the marketplace without connection to a large corporation and with informal relationships to many branches and denominations of faith.

We like it best when people buy our books from booksellers, our partners in successfully reaching as wide an audience as possible.

What We Are Doing
Books

Paraclete Press publishes books that show the richness and depth of what it means to be Christian. Although Benedictine spirituality is at the heart of all that we do, we publish books that reflect the Christian experience across many cultures, time periods, and houses of worship.

We publish books that nourish the vibrant life of the church and its people—books about spiritual practice, formation, history, ideas, and customs.

We have several different series of books within Paraclete Press, including the bestselling Living Library series of modernized classic texts; A Voice from the Monastery—giving voice to men and women monastics about what it means to live a spiritual life today; award-winning literary faith fiction; and books that explore Judaism and Islam and discover how these faiths inform Christian thought and practice.

Recordings

From Gregorian chant to contemporary American choral works, our music recordings celebrate the richness of sacred choral music through the centuries. Paraclete is proud to distribute the recordings of the internationally acclaimed choir Gloriæ Dei Cantores, who have been praised for their "rapt and fathomless spiritual intensity" by *American Record Guide*, and the Gloriæ Dei Cantores Schola, which specializes in the study and performance of Gregorian chant. Paraclete is also the exclusive North American distributor of the recordings of the Monastic Choir of St. Peter's Abbey in Solesmes, France, long considered to be a leading authority on Gregorian chant performance.

Learn more about us at our website:
www.paracletepress.com, or call us toll-free at
1-800-451-5006.

First Fruits of Prayer
A Forty-Day Journey
through the Canon of St. Andrew

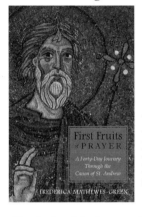

Frederica Mathewes-Green
ISBN 13: 978-1-55725-469-6
238 pages
$19.95, Trade paper

Join **Frederica Mathewes-Green** on a guided retreat—ideal for the Lenten season—through the classic Great Canon, a wise, ancient, Orthodox text that will enrich your experience of prayer. Regardless of your denominational background, *First Fruits of Prayer* will bring to life the experience of first-millenium Christianity through immersion in some of their most vital spiritual practices.

> "This is destined to become a devotional classic
> for generations to come."
> —*Dallas Morning News*

> "If you want to read something that will challenge you and
> -deepen your relationship with God...this is the book."
> —*Episcopal Life*

Available from most booksellers or through Paraclete Press:
www.paracletepress.com
1-800-451-5006 • Try your local bookstore first.